Contemporary Theatre and the Christian Faith

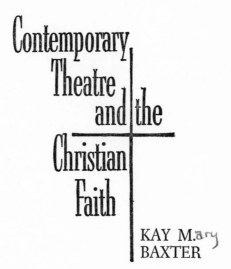

Contemporary Theatre and the Christian Faith

KAY M. BAXTER

Abingdon Press—new york • nashville

CONTEMPORARY THEATRE AND THE CHRISTIAN FAITH

Published in England by the SCM Press
under the title of SPEAK WHAT WE FEEL.
© SCM Press Ltd. 1964
All rights reserved.

Library of Congress Catalog Card Number: 65-21976

The selections on pages 79, 80, 83 are reprinted by permission of S. G. Phillips, Inc., from *Look Back in Anger* by John Osborne. Copyright © 1957 by S. G. Phillips, Inc.

Theater – moral and religious aspects

SET UP, PRINTED, AND BOUND BY THE
PARTHENON PRESS, AT NASHVILLE,
TENNESSEE, UNITED STATES OF AMERICA

PREFACE

No theatre is new. But today's theatre is concerned, more deeply than for many generations, with exploring the human condition in all its aspects. Inevitably it touches at many points upon the concerns of thoughtful Christians. In both theatre and church there is a ferment of dissatisfaction and a thrust of hope. The aim of this short book is to observe the points at which the "new" theatre can illuminate some of the problems which Christians face in understanding and communicating their faith.

The book is a revised and abbreviated version of a series of lectures delivered in 1959 and 1963 to students of Union Theological Seminary, New York, during the presidency of Dr. H. P. van Dusen and through the introduction of Mr. E. Martin Browne. The lectures formed part of the drama course directed by Dr. Robert Seaver, and I am deeply indebted to faculty and to students for the opportunity and joy of those periods of residence among them.

There are many others, both scholarly and devout, in

theatre and in church circles, to whose encouragement thanks are due, but because this essay is the work of an amateur both of drama and of Christianity, they would probably prefer not to have their names publicly associated with it. Any credit is theirs; any error or heresy all my own work.

K.M.B.

CONTENTS

1
WAITING IN THE
LIVING ROOM

Two Plays about the Human Condition

> All the dead voices
>   They make a sound like wings
> Like leaves
>   Like sand . . .

On January 5, 1953, in Paris, in a ramshackle playhouse now demolished, all the dead voices fell silent, and a new voice was heard in the theatre. The theatre is still exploring the possibilities of the new instrument created by Samuel Beckett, in the play *En Attendant Godot*.[1] The play was written in French, the Irish author being then resident in France, and subsequently translated by the author for the London production of 1955. Beckett is reported as having said that if he had intended the word Godot to mean God he would have written God. To Anglo-Saxon ears the two words are easy of association. But in French, as Ronald Gray has pointed out in a BBC talk, the words nearest in sound to Godot are *godenot, godichon, godelureau, godasses*— "runt, lout, clumsy bumpkin, clumsy boots"—all words indicating the opposite of what we mean by Godlike. Martin Esslin is probably correct in attributing it to Beckett's recol-

[1] *Waiting for Godot,* written and translated by Samuel Beckett (Evergreen ed. New York: Grove Press, 1956). For the background, see J. Guicharnaud and J. Beckelman, *Modern French Theatre,* Yale University Press, 1961.

9

lection of an early farce in which characters wait for one "Godeau." [2]

In the play two tramps are found in a lane outside a city. Beside them on a mound is a tree of sorrow, a death tree. The time is evening. All day the tramps have been separated. Now, reunited, they wait for the arrival of a mysterious Mr. Godot, who, if he comes as they think he has promised to come, will put everything right in their lives and tell them what to do to keep everything right. The tramps are called Vladimir and Estragon, nicknamed Didi and Gogo. Vladimir, as the reader will no doubt remember, is the name of that saint of the Russian Orthodox church who was so eager to discover and follow "the best religion" that he sent messengers all over the known world to bring him news of all the forms of religion there were. Estragon, as one finds by using a French dictionary and a botanical reference book, is French for tarragon, and tarragon is not only used for vinegar, but is also a plant of the family *cruciferae,* and *cruciferae* means cross-bearers. If you prefer to identify the tramps through symbols stemming from Jung's psychology, you will note that Didi-Vladimir wears a hat, which does not become him, i.e., is concerned with uncomfortable thought, and Gogo-Estragon wears boots which don't fit him, i.e., is concerned with uncomfortable feeling. If you want to identify them in terms of the religious life you can say that Didi is the contemplative, the listener, the seeker, the one expecting messages, the ascetic, the one who suppresses his physical side, while Gogo is the active, the nonreflective, the one who tries to

[2] See Martin Esslin, *Theatre of the Absurd* (Anchor Books ed. New York: Doubleday & Co., 1962).

wipe the tears from the eyes of sufferers, who must eat when he is hungry, and who bellows when he is hurt. Neither can do without the other. The play opens with their discussion of life, while they wait. Beckett conveys to the audience that their life is a pretty futile affair. For Godot, toward whom their attitude is to say the least ambiguous, doesn't come. And time passes.

At last, two travelers appear, a coarse blustering brute called Pozzo, finely dressed and obviously pampered, and his attendant, a starveling object called Lucky. Lucky is tied to Pozzo by a cord, is driven on by a whip, and is loaded down with Pozzo's luggage. Pozzo yells at him, but he remains mute, doesn't react when hit, and seems indifferent to the fact that the cord around his neck has rubbed a sore. After some exchanges—in which Pozzo finds great amusement in reflecting that he himself *and* the tramps are of the same species, "made in God's image"—Pozzo settles to eat some food (chicken sandwiches), allowing the tramps to have the bones. It becomes clear that in spite of his braggadocio Pozzo is really quite helpless without his "menial," as he calls him. He says, however, that he can no longer endure Lucky and is going to take him to market and see what he can get for him there. In the French version the name of the market, or fair, is Saint Sauveur. Like most people with something to sell, Pozzo extols Lucky's abilities, and, to show him off, makes Gogo and Didi ask him to think and to dance. The only dance Lucky can now perform (though Pozzo says he was once a wonderful dancer, dancing for pure happiness) is a dance of death. Pozzo says "Make him think," and Lucky obediently begins to think aloud, his hat fallen off, and his spare white

11

locks falling about his skull. He makes a long speech of no obvious coherence, and seems to be suffering so intensely that Gogo attempts to wipe his tears, but he wounds Gogo with a kick.

After two full pages of soliloquy which is often regarded as incomprehensible balderdash Lucky is set upon by the tramps—and indeed the audience itself is nearly ready to set upon him by this time. Attacked and falling down, Lucky appears to die. At this point Pozzo finds he has lost his watch. Time stops altogether. There is a terrible stench as of corpses. Pozzo says, "I must go." E.: "And your half-hunter?" P.: "I must have left it at the manor." E.: "Then Adieu." P.: "Adieu." V.: "Adieu. . . ." P.: "I don't seem able to . . . depart." E.: "Such is life."

Such is life; although we all say *Adieu,* "To God," we can't go there. At last, however, in a sequence to which we shall return, Pozzo gets Lucky on to his feet again and they go off to the designated market to see what he will fetch there. The tramps are again alone. A messenger, a boy, who says that though not of those parts he yet belongs here, comes to say that Mr. Godot won't come this evening but surely tomorrow. The tramps continue to wait. The curtain descends; the play is half over.

Now what, in the world or out of it, is all this about? Have patience and press on, more rapidly, through Part II. Part II begins exactly as before except that (a) the tree has put forth leaves, (b) Gogo's boots have been put off and are left in the center of the stage and with them Lucky's hat, and (c) Didi is alone, singing a sad circular comic song about a dog who died as an example to others! Gogo turns up, the tramps express their affection for each other, and

12

then quarrel again, chiefly about time, about *when* things happen, or happened, or will happen, for time has got into a confusion since Pozzo and Lucky went off the stage. The two tramps make up their quarrel, however, realizing neither can do without the other, and, to pass the time, play at being Pozzo and Lucky, in particular trying to imitate Lucky's last dance. They call it "doing the tree" and they are quite unsuccessful. This is one of several semicomic, semiserious ritual actions which they perform. They stagger about, and at last Estragon cries out: "God have pity on me." "And me?" says Vladimir, "what about *me?*" "On me! On me!" cries Estragon. "God have pity on *me!*"

It is impossible to convey the intensity of their cry over such an apparently trivial failure. But immediately the cry is uttered Pozzo and Lucky reappear. Pozzo is now blind; Lucky as before but wearing a new hat. Lucky goes directly to the foot of the tree and lies there inert, apparently sleeping. The tramps argue awhile with Pozzo, who then asks: "Who are you?" They answer: "We are men." Pozzo, struggling to follow to where Lucky lies asleep, falls, cannot rise, and calls for help. The tramps ask: "What is his name?" They try him with the name: "Abel!" He responds: "Help!" They call: "Cain!" Again Pozzo replies: "Help!" They say: "He's all mankind." "All Mankind"—and the name he is given by Beckett? Pozzo, the Fool.

During the interchanges that follow Pozzo reveals that whereas "before," i.e., in Part I or the "first time," he thought he had such wonderful sight, now he knows he is blind and fears he has reached a place called the Board where he may be "up for trial." The tramps reassure him that he is still only "at the tree." Lucky wakes, *rises,* and prepares to lead Pozzo off, this time not towards the market but back towards the city. There are further arguments between the tramps and then Didi sums up. A second messenger comes to say Mr. Godot won't be coming that evening and the play peters out in a continuance of the futile exchanges of the two tramps, who agree that suicide is probably what they will commit, but not this evening, tomorrow perhaps. In Gogo's words: "Nothing happens, no one comes, no one goes, it's awful."

Opinions about the play have naturally varied very much in different countries. Is it, as many people thought and think, an attempt to see just how gullible an audience can be? It is difficult, at such a level, to explain the extraordinary attraction, the holding power, of the dialogue, or the fact that one's frame of mind at the end is radically different from one's frame of mind at the start. Moreover, the beautifully balanced structure of the play, which becomes clear if the thesis now put forward is accepted, is a structure too honest for deceit.

What is meant by its structure? Isn't it just two lengths of string—just a meaningless shapeless straggle of dialogue? Not in the view of at least one member of the audience.

Serious examination will show that the deep structure of the play is that of a passion play, in which the whole, perfectly orthodox, scheme of redemption is played out before our eyes. The play's synopsis is "Came down, was crucified, dead, buried, descended into hell and the third day rose, and ascended."

This does not by any means prove that Beckett is a crypto-Christian—or that he is attempting to write religious drama of the Eliot kind. But he *is* giving us his reaction to his experience of the story of the Passion. Let us accept the partial identification of the waiting tramps as the praying soul (let us add, in its two aspects of active and contemplative).[3] The tramps together are the spirit of man. The spirit is spasmodically attentive and expectant of a Saviour. The Saviour comes as it was foretold ". . . without form or comeliness" (*Godichon, godenot*), "despised and rejected," "despised and we esteemed him not." He comes carrying Pozzo's rubbishy gear; "He hath borne our griefs and carried our sorrows:" wounded, bruised, afflicted yet dumb, suffering yet without threats, "making his grave with the wicked and with the rich in his death." He is to have "a portion divided with the great and shall divide the spoils with the strong"—yes, even if it is only a picnic and the bones of a chicken. The biblical description of the Suffering Servant (Isa. 53) fits in every detail the figure of Lucky, this servant of the gross Pozzo who represents all mankind. And is it hard to agree that "Lucky" is quite a good modern translation of *Beatus*, "the Blessed One," adding to the traditional appellation a twist of sardonic humor apt to our times?

This servant, Lucky, is done to death at the tree, at a place where constant reference is made to a skull. This section can be taken in several ways but it seems that the death takes place in the mind of man. Vladimir the thinker seems less affected by the agony of Lucky than is Estragon the sensual man. It is the agony of mind to which we are made witness. Pozzo bears testimony to the fact that it is when Lucky *thinks* that he finds Lucky intolerable. Now

[3] *Times Literary Supplement,* February 10, 1956.

15

this is not only interesting because it is in the intellectual acceptance of redemption that many of us find our greatest difficulty. It is also interesting because Beckett is concerned to portray man's will to the crucifixion of God as a state of mind. In the great death speech of Lucky, when you have removed the nonsense-pieces and have retained only the major statements in the speech, you have something like this: *Given the existence of a personal God who loves us and suffers and considering that, as a result of labors left unfinished, man wastes and pines—I resume, in a word, the skull.*

The tramps and Pozzo have earlier pointed out that the servant's suffering is quite voluntary; he has power to take up or to lay down his way of life. Having made the statement, Lucky *appears to die.* "In the sight of the unwise" he seems to die and his "departure is taken for misery." Pozzo, helpless without his servant, exclaims over the body, "Raise him up!" They ask each other what to do and Estragon says "to hell with him"—and to hell, presumably to the harrowing thereof, Lucky "departs," accompanied by Pozzo, for whom time has stopped. It is, for Pozzo, the end of what the playwright calls the *First Time,* and is expressed dramatically by making Pozzo lose his gold watch. In the timeless interval the tramps cannot trace the sequence of their past history, memory goes adrift, and Pozzo, on his return journey, when questioned gets angry and says: "Why ask 'when' about everything? Everything's the same."

However, when the second act begins everything is very definitely not the same. Vladimir, who has only thought about what has happened, opens the scene with the dirge for the dead dog, and is worried about the absence of Estragon. Where is Estragon? Estragon's boots are left empty in the center of the stage and with them Lucky's discarded hat. In some sense, partially, are we to understand that Estragon has died with Lucky? His movement of compassion towards Lucky in Lucky's agony, the movement which caused him however unpremeditatedly to incur the wound Lucky inflicted on him—the mystic's Wound of Love?—this action of Estragon's has certainly resulted in a change of feeling for him. His feet are now freed from the painful boots, and another change is in the tree. In Act I it was dead. Now it has suddenly put forth leaves; from being a death-place the mound now bears a tree of life. How not, when hell has been harrowed, the souls ransomed and the Suffering Servant become the first fruits of them that slept?

Here attention should be directed to Beckett's sensitive use of a device to stress this point about the tree's symbolism. He gives the tramps the beautiful lyric:

Estragon: All the dead voices.
Vladimir: They make a noise like wings.
Estragon: Like leaves.
Vladimir: Like sand.
Estragon: Like leaves . . .
Vladimir: They make a noise like feathers.
Estragon: Like leaves.
Vladimir: Like ashes.
Estragon: Like leaves.

They are quarreling, as usual, when the lyric seems quietly to come into being. The force of the passage is greatly enhanced by the presence of the stark tree now lightly touched with foliage, but its real quality is in the movement of voices, mood sifting down through sense.

When time begins again at Pozzo's return, Pozzo explains his newly won knowledge of his own blindness. This knowledge is the only trophy he has brought back from his journey to the fair, the place of exchange—the place called Saint Sauveur. Is there a better symbol of redemption than to know our blindness and be forced to accept our dependence on Christ? While, then, the redeemed Pozzo is speaking of this knowledge, Lucky sleeps at the foot of the tree, now become the Tree of Life, and it is only when Lucky *rises* that Pozzo, now totally dependent, can move under Lucky's guidance towards the city whence they two originally came. The tramps remain; for them the significance of what has happened is not clear, as Didi, in his final big speech, reveals.

Didi says, as he watches the sleeping Estragon, and in saying this perhaps indicates the root sin of our generation:

> Was I sleeping, while the others suffered? Am I sleeping now? Tomorrow, when I wake, or think I do, what shall I say of today? That with Estragon, my friend, at this place, until the fall of night, I waited for Godot? That Pozzo passed, with his carrier, and talked to us? Probably. But in all that what truth will there be? . . . Astride of a grave and a difficult birth. Down in the hole, lingeringly, the grave-digger puts on the forceps. We have time to grow old. . . .

"Astride of a grave, and a difficult birth." Does not this, in modern terminology, sum up singularly well the meaning of "descended into hell and the third day rose again"?

To work through the play thinking along these lines reveals, not, certainly, a line for line parallel to the scriptural story of the Passion, but nevertheless a crucifixion, deposition, descent into hell, resurrection and ascension, deeply pondered upon and perfectly scaled to the limits imposed by modern theatrical convention. After seeing *Godot,* playwrights can never approach the theme of the Passion in the same way as they approached it before. It is not, of course, in any sense a *rendering* of the Gospel story. To compare Dorothy L. Sayers' *The Man Born to Be King* with Beckett would be like comparing children's colored cut-outs with an El Greco. They exist in totally different dimensions of being.

What is given, if you enter at all fully into the part of the play concerned with Lucky, is a sense that here is total suffering. One enters into the increasing desperation, the attempt to communicate meaning through and in despite of all the catch phrases of the day, against the dead weight of words loaded with horror, the great cold, the great dark, the place of stones. One is aware of the constant vibration of the will to fulfill the accepted task, the face set like a flint to Jerusalem—and in the constantly repeated "I resume" (which means at once "I take again," "I summarize in myself," "I embody") we hear the Word of God, incarnate and bound within a dying skull, in the place called Golgotha, which is, being translated, "The place of the skull." All this we hear, and at the last, not the comfortable word upon which Christians lean every Good Friday, not the breathed "It is finished" of the perfected offering, but the searing recognition that only by such suffering can the labors left unfinished be accomplished and man cease to waste and pine. To sleep while such suffering is endured is to deny Christ. Is not this a poignant commentary upon Paul's mysterious words about the vocation of Christians to fill up the sufferings of Christ?

Perhaps it calls in question the impassibility of the Deity but certainly we know that one of the names of God is *Immanuel,* God with us, and in an age of desolation and grief this interpretation of the Suffering Servant is one which grips an audience with extraordinary power. And if it is true that in meditating on the Passion all that enlightens and enlarges the understanding is to be welcomed, then to think, as this play forces one to think, of God as entered into the pain *we* endure in knowing the neverendingness of the work of salvation, is to think with strength at a point where thought often breaks down into mere emotion.

The interchange following Lucky's death-fall is characteristic of the "doublespeak" which conveys the many leveled implications of this intensely wrought work. *Lucky falls.* "Raise him up!" This is not only the straightforward plea for help in lifting the body, but the heart-cry of all mankind seeing its Saviour destroyed. "He's doing it on purpose!" at once corroborates the voluntary nature of the sacrifice and voices the childish hope that it is only a pretend-death, not a real one. "You must hold him." The incarnate God has surrendered himself into the power of mankind his creature. "To hell with him!" Yes, of course, we had forgotten (but our author had not) that the labors are unfinished while souls are to ransom from hell. And what is the effect upon the onlooking soul? Do we get any hint of an answer to Vladimir's first thoughtful observation that

20

there were two thieves and only one was saved? There is a hint of an answer at two points. The first comes towards the end of Act I. There is no sun but the moon sheds a pale light on the scene. Estragon has his boots off, one in each hand.

> *Vladimir:* Your boots. What are you doing with your boots?
> *Estragon:* I'm leaving them there. Another will come just as . . . we are, but with smaller feet and they'll make him happy.
> *V.:* But you can't go barefoot.
> *E.:* Christ did.
> *V.:* Christ! What's Christ got to do with it? You're not going to compare yourself with Christ!
> *E.:* All my life I've compared myself with Christ.
> *V.:* But where he was it was warm, it was dry.
> *E.:* Yes, and they crucified quick.

It is a glimpse—only a brief hint. To be prepared to be "crucified . . . quick"—is that the acid test of discipleship? The hint is picked up again in the second part in one of those absurd pieces of apparently aimless cross talk between the two.

> *V.:* . . . but we could have done without it.
> *E.: Que voulez-vous?*
> *V.:* I beg your pardon.
> *E.: Que voulez-vous?*
> *V.:* Ah! *Que voulez-vous?* Exactly.

Exactly. What do you *will?* For understand that salvation concerns the *will.*

Possibly the clue to what has happened to Estragon is

shown in his change of boots. He offered his boots, his sense-life, and *willed* to go barefoot like Christ. But then he found a different pair of boots, and instead of remembering his will, he just stepped into someone else's way of feeling—and so, perhaps lost his chance? Or perhaps even the most painful boots, the worst pains, can be endured once the will lies easy in the hand of God?

To conclude: If you listen to this play with your spirit as well as with your ears, cross-referencing Testaments, church history, personal religious life, the commonplaces of psychological theory, what you know of the world's pains, and the actual text itself, with all the connotations of the words, you will find that, far from complaining that the play moves too slowly, you will hardly have time to respond to each brief phrase as it falls from the lips of the immobile actors and you will find that you have food for thought for many days. It must be reiterated, however, that the author must not be supposed to be writing from an orthodox Christian point of view. He is merely moving, and living, and recording experience within the structure of the Christian story.

Graham Greene's play *The Living Room* [4] presents a contrast. Some points of comparison with Beckett are at once obvious. We know that Beckett, who had an ordinary upper-middle-class education in Ireland and subsequently lived for many years in France, is certain to have, deeply rooted in his consciousness, visual symbols of the persons of the Trinity, and a firm grasp of the structure of orthodox Christian tenets. Whatever may be Beckett's present posi-

[4] (New York: The Viking Press, 1954.)

tion, he was brought up under the imagined eye of that dread God-with-a-white-beard (whom the tramp Estragon, be it noted, *does not* identify with Godot) who is said to send messengers from on high into a world from which God himself is remote. This absence of God (the root theme of the existentialists following the philosopher Heidegger) conditions all the thinking of Beckett. Indeed it is part of the data of most serious postwar plays, and Beckett is at pains to make us understand that the tramps—all of us poor benighted Would-Be-Goods—are looking for God in the wrong direction.

Where does Graham Greene look for God? His background is that of a fully instructed Roman Catholic. The characters in *The Living Room* are (all but Michael Dennis) professing Roman Catholics. The morality which determines their actions is one which they base, however mistakenly, on what they understand of Catholic doctrine. Why has Greene chosen such a melodramatic story? Rose, a young orphan, is to become part of the household of her uncle James, a priest crippled years earlier by an accident. He lives with his two sisters, the girl's aunts, both spinsters; Teresa is senile and Helen is half-crazy. These three live in a house where they have shut and locked the doors of any room in which anyone has died. The senile Teresa is so guilt-ridden about her own body that she pretends to be invisible as she goes in and out of the lavatory, and Helen wields over Teresa the weapon of pretending Teresa will go mad if she acts against her younger sister's wishes. Rose, the orphan who is to live with this dreadful trio, has just fallen passionately in love with the executor of her dead father's will, Michael Dennis, who is early middle aged and married to a neurotic wife. Dennis is flattered by the young girl's adoration of him, but lacks the courage either to break with his wife or to give up Rose. The action takes place entirely in the top floor living room.

What was Greene's aim? The conflict which should, we are always told, be in the very center of a play, is not in this play very clearly defined, although it is a solidly constructed play, well outside the plotlessness of the "theatre of the absurd." In the play as in life, the pulls go in several directions at once, involving several different relationships. Will Rose defy convention and her church and run off with Dennis? Will Dennis break with his wife? Will either of the sisters take some drastic step to prevent Rose's escape? Will James be galvanized into action when one of the most rigid rules of his church—that against divorce—seems likely to be disregarded by souls for whom he cannot but feel some responsibility? Or will Dennis' wife precipitate a crisis? The play vibrates, in the first half, with all these genuinely theatrical possibilities.

It is a brilliant idea. Into the faded, loveless, futile climate created by the three old horrors upstairs, who are the product (Greene is at pains to show) of adherence to a sterile formalist religious practice, he brings the vivid innocent eroticism of Rose, who has responded without a thought of right or wrong to the love which she imagines Dennis to be offering, at the moment of her bereavement, to her hitherto unawakened heart. Rose, at her first appearance on stage, brings into a sordid demoralized group the stimulus of a perfectly pure soul. For her, the fact of Dennis' adultery doesn't really exist. She cannot envisage it—it is miles outside her experience. And this innocence is delineated by Greene with delicacy, precision, and economy. Whether or not her name was chosen because of Blake's wild and heartrending poem, that poem summarizes her fate.

> O Rose, thou art sick,
> The invisible worm
> That flies in the night
> In the howling storm
> Has found out thy bed
> Of crimson joy
> And his dark secret love
> Doth thy life destroy.

Rose loves, then, without counting the cost. But her frail romance withers all too soon. The hotel assignations, the clandestine hours stolen with Dennis, are already showing themselves for what they are—tawdry and blasphemous counterfeits of real love. When she sees, for the first time, her lover and his wife together, she realizes with tragic suddenness that a marriage exists between them—a real, an irreversible relationship. The cry *"They are married!"* which breaks from her is an involuntary recognition of a fact—a recognition of an unalterable state. Whom God hath joined together no man *can* put asunder—and it is this recognition which shatters the radiance of her dream in a way no argument could shatter it. Greene has compressed into this one anguished cry of Rose's the whole Catholic doctrine of the irreversible nature of matrimony as sacrament. It is infinitely more convincing than are the subsequent discussions.

In Dennis, Greene shows us a weakly selfish, middle-aged

man, wanting the rejuvenation of a young love, but unwilling to pay the price, in his own or in his wife's life, to secure his "freedom." He knows he will never really be quit of his wife, the effort would be too great, and the wife's selfishness, equal to his own, will hold him to a loveless contract by any means, fair or foul, which she can employ. Clearly, one of the things Greene is concerned to say is that freedom is not a question of circumstances or of rules, but of the *will* (*Que voulez-vous?*), and the way to freedom, in Eliot's words:

Is prayer, observance, discipline, thought and action.

The weakness of the play is that no character in it is prepared even to *try* to follow this austere path. When the pains of life press in upon them, they all escape, either upstairs to the next floor, or into a bath chair, or into clandestine flirtations, or into hysterics, or, finally, in Rose's case, into death itself.

Rose, as was inevitable, kills herself with the overdose of sedative tablets Marion Dennis has been prevented from taking. She dies in a particularly touching situation, because she has in vain put out hands for help both to her uncle and to her aunt. The morning after Rose's death, Dennis and the crippled priest James have a final conversation in which Greene gives us, one must suppose, his own summary of the play's theme.

Dennis asks, rather whiningly: "What is this God whose laws not only cause but condition such hideous pain to creation?" And James gives the stock Christian answer: "None of us loves enough." Our crucifixions, Greene wishes to say, are not arranged by God. We crucify each other. The Christian vocation, open to everyone, priest or layman, is the vocation to enter into the mystery of suffering, and to *be with* the sufferer. James says that God gave him thirty years of deprivation in a wheel chair to learn this elementary lesson of the spiritual life and he never tried to learn it. So that, at the end of the play when God "flings a suffering child" at his feet crying for help, he is dumb. This is *our* sin, not the act of a pitiless Creator. Power to release comes only from power to endure. No birth without death. Is not this, really, the conclusion which Vladimir reaches in *Godot*? (As we shall see, it certainly is Clov's conclusion in Beckett's *Endgame*.)

But one can assume that Greene sees a great deal deeper than he allows either Dennis or James to see, and that this deeper insight is expressed in a kind of subplot, through the relationship of the two aunts, the servant Mary, and Rose.

Look again at the symbols which Greene uses. In the tall decaying house of life, room after room is shut as person after person dies from among those who hold these three old people by slender threads to the living world. They do indeed depend on each other but not through any creative desire for each other's fulfillment, only to preserve as far as they can the *status quo ante*. Their attitude towards their servant, Mary, is all of a piece with this lack of love. Mary is a thing, as much an object for their use as is the tray she carries. So, shrinking more and more from the openness which real life, life eternal, demands, they have climbed to the top story of the house—i.e., symbolically as far as possible from the world with its earthly feet. They are beleaguered there in their tower room, inescapably up against the fact that the next move, for one or other of them, is the move into the unmentionable—into death.

Into this horrible trap—this cobwebby bottle if you like—is poured, with Rose's arrival, the new wine, the ferment of new life and new love. Two of the old people, Helen and James, are too far lost to respond at all to what Rose means. It is only Teresa, the senile, the nearest to death, who does touch life again through Rose's coming, and this she does because in her weak ineffectual dazed way she allows herself to love Rose. She lets Rose help her, and through Rose's death loses her own fear of anything, even of her own terrifying sister. Nor is the strength Rose's coming gives to Teresa a strength only to face death. Teresa's attitude is not only that if Rose could die, death cannot be so dreadful.

> Have not little children gone,
> And Lesbia's sparrow, all alone?

No. It is more than this. Teresa is strengthened by the fact that Rose, by staying to care for her when she was ill, gave expression to love—the real thing, not the illusion of it which Rose herself thought to find with Dennis, and Greene is showing in this last minute rally of Teresa's strength that this action of Rose's proves *to Teresa* that Teresa has value. She matters—and her restored value gives power to withstand the fear of Helen, and ultimately the fear of death. She thus in her tired, fluttering way bears her straw of testimony to the real nature of love. The sub-plot amplifies and saves from banality the rather glib phrase about not loving enough, which Greene puts into the mouth of James.

This play is a very powerful one, a fine example of how a gifted and practiced writer can create tensions which, like a game of cat's cradle, resolve into each other only to create the next group of tensions.

And yet—and yet—how does one explain the uneasy feeling that it is not fully Christian in its basic assumptions?

Partly the uneasiness is due to the presence, at the end, of too many statements, made by James the priest, which sound (as he says himself) like the Penny Catechism: partly because Greene has weighted the dice so heavily against the good that we cannot quite believe in the situation—one feels that in real life *some* secular power for good would have been available for one or other of the characters to grab hold of, though it is possible that Greene deliberately cut this out to show what happens if you *do* withdraw from life's responsibilities. But there is one further reason for reacting away from the play, even while recognizing its good qualities.

When Henry Vaughan's words come to us out of the seventeenth century

> Dear, beauteous death, the jewel of the just,
> Shining nowhere but in the dark

we accept the language. It is the authentic language of an elderly saint writing of his friends departed; longing only to rejoin them.

This is acceptable; but when one is asked, with the body of a dead child, self-destroyed, still in the house, to assent to the statement "Death is our child—we have to go

29

through pain to bear our death—Rose is free, she has borne her child," some instinct says firmly either "this is nonsense" or "it's pernicious, morbid blasphemy." Rose was done to death by the cruelty surrounding her, working on her own weakness and ignorance. Far from having "borne her child" (except in the sense perhaps of having brought a kind of redemption to poor Teresa), Rose has been forever cheated of life, utterly against the will of God who gave her life. Greene does, here as at times in his novels, seem to say that a capacity to despair is a sign, almost, of special grace. He courts the dark night of the soul, and there is something almost arrogant in this attitude towards life. Estragon, in *Godot*, is a truer picture of the family of *Cruciferae* or crossbearers. Compassion drives Estragon to share suffering but he yells vigorously when through his compassionate act he incurs the wound of love. Estragon is on healthier ground when in response to Vladimir's suggestion that they might try repenting he replies, in all innocence, "Of what? Repent of being born?"

Somehow, in Greene's play, the experience is not fully rounded out. The ending does not satisfy. Perhaps a kind of compunction restrained him? The giants do not yield to the promptings of compunction, as a brief glance at the endings of Lear or of Hamlet will show.

Lear cries out, over the body of the dead innocent Cordelia:

Why should a dog, a horse, a rat, have life
And thou no breath at all?

and the terrible scene closes with Albany speaking the tag line:

The weight of this sad time we must obey,
Speak what we feel, not what we ought to say.

It is a moment when to moralize is to commit an indecency.

The same remote grandeur broods over the ending of *Hamlet*, with the entry of Fortinbras, and Horatio's last utterance:

Then let me speak to the yet unknowing world
Of carnal, bloody, and unnatural acts,
Of accidental judgments, casual slaughters,
And, in this upshot, purposes mistook.

There is no place, in the last hours of such a tragedy, for preaching: only for a last entering into the mistaken purpose, the accidental judgment and the casual slaughter, so as to enlarge the capacity for wonder, the knowledge of what the spirit of man is capable of doing and suffering. "Speak what we feel, not what we ought to say." It is, among many other reasons, because Beckett habitually fulfills Albany's injunction, that his claims to excellence are so far above those of Graham Greene.

The two plays considered—Beckett's wholly involved, Graham Greene's weakened by a didactic streak—serve at least to bring to light some of the questions which perplex today's playwrights.

Is God's will made clear to those who meditate on the mystery of suffering? Is salvation a matter of the will? Is God's name Immanuel, or is he the great Absentee? Who are the messengers of God—the clergy? or the "clumsy boots"? Does the church any longer mediate salvation to sinners? If not, who are the mediators? What is sin? Are

31

we to understand that the whole human trail of suffering could be avoided if people acted according to the light they have? The tramps could have carried Pozzo's luggage and eased Lucky's pains, Pozzo could have shared his food, the Living Room's inhabitants could have loved the two erring lovers and the neurotic wife back into spiritual health. Could they? Are we called to be Christ to our neighbors or is the task really beyond us all? Is all this what the authors are saying? Or are they in fact as much in the dark as the characters they portray?

Many of the most worthwhile plays of our time are written by honest, deeply thinking, deeply feeling writers who have not been able to get further than asking the questions, and who refuse to be put off with cheap and shallow answers, or even with answers of great profundity if they cannot understand what is being said. The main task of Christian students of drama is to build bridges, and if we are to be any use in building a communications line between the artist and the church and in making the insights of the seers available to deepen our own shallow thinking, let alone if we are going to be any help to the artists in their search for the unknown God, then we have to get in beside them and understand the nature of their trouble, being prepared to bar no questions.

In the twentieth-century theatre, the decline of religious belief produces a problem which neither Greek nor medieval writer had to face. Both Greeks and medievals could count on an audience, not indeed highbrow, but well versed in the stories and the assumptions from which the dramatist started, and on which he could lean. Our dramatists today can count on no common background—witness the slowness of critics, whether professional or amateur, in recognizing the identity of the suffering Servant Lucky, without which *Godot* really makes nonsense. Christian arguments or allusions are not commonly understood.

On the other hand, the contemporary theatre offers Christians an enrichment of which they are not nearly enough aware. Even those of us who think we believe with the simple faith of our forbears deceive ourselves. We cannot contract out of our environment. The great changes in that environment since the Renaissance can be disregarded only at our peril. Writers, like artists of other kinds, are constantly engaged in trying to assimilate and make their own the findings of all who are studying what man was, or is, or is to be. The findings of astronomers, anthropologists, psychologists, neurologists, and biochemists, no less then the findings of the economists and politicians, are all relevant to the enlarged understanding of the psalmist's question: "What is Man, that thou art mindful of him?" Gradually these findings are expressed in drama—and thus can enrich the ancient doctrines of the church.

Brecht's *Galileo* [5] provides an example of how a playwright—even one for whom personally the conclusion is atheism—can reach across the frontier between the theatre (and the world) and the church. For *Galileo* expresses in drama what the church's own theologians are struggling to say to the world about the God who is met in the depths of contemporary experience, not in "religion" or "in the sky" or "out there." Brecht shows the shock to traditional faith.

[5] In *Plays*, 2 vols. Reprinted by permission of Random House, Inc., Methuen & Co., Ltd., and Suhrkamp Verlag.

In the play the monk speaks of his aged and uneducated parents, and asks:

> How could they take it, were I to tell them that they are on a lump of stone ceaselessly spinning in empty space, circling around a second-rate star? What, then, would be the use of their patience, their acceptance of misery?

The old cardinal also protests:

> I am informed that Mr. Galileo transfers mankind from the centre of the universe to somewhere on the outskirts. Mr. Galileo is therefore an enemy of mankind and must be dealt with as such. Is it conceivable that God would trust this most precious fruit of his labour to a minor frolicking star . . .? I won't have it! I won't have it! I won't be a nobody on an inconsequential star briefly twirling hither and thither.

Sagredo, the religious believer, on being told that there are stars revolving around Jupiter, and that there are no crystal spheres supporting the heavens, confesses himself afraid:

> *Sagredo:* What do you think is going to happen to you for saying that there is another sun around which other earths revolve? And that there are only stars and no difference between earth and heaven? Where is God then?
> *Galileo:* What do you mean?
> *Sagredo:* God? Where is God?
> *Galileo:* Not there! Any more than he'd be here—if creatures from the moon came down to look for him.
> *Sagredo:* Then where is he? . . . Where is God in your system of the universe?
> *Galileo:* Within ourselves. Or—nowhere.

It is possible that we are at the moment in a phase of drama genuinely antipathetic to the Christian doctrine which seeks to explain the God who is found "within ourselves" (as there is certainly a considerable antipathy among the new dramatists to the *intellectual* life, or at least to any verbal statement of intellectual problems). And there is a bleak neutral strip between Christian and non-Christian when it comes to the discussion of the meaning of the new theatre. Few playgoers tolerate the kind of *Godot*-analysis which has just been presented. Few humanists can endure the idea that truth is sometimes uttered through the cryptogram. In his *Theatre of the Absurd* Martin Esslin refers to these sequences as "Routines," relating them to the clown's routines in the circus. The critic who tries to relate what is being said in the theatre today with the doctrines of the Christian faith exposes himself, inevitably, to the jibe that there are *some* people who think *Three Blind Mice* is a cryptogram about the Trinity.

Let the jibe swing on! No one has yet explained the fascination the clown cross talk has, or asked why the human vein pulses more strongly after a transfusion of nonsense. But there are some grounds for believing that ritual is the therapy man has devised for canalizing his wild irrationality into safe limits. Neither the experiments of Reinhardt in mass-theatre nor the stadium evangelism of Billy Graham have provided the answer, but they have led audiences toward the question of how to effect the communal ritual acceptance of *guilt* and release. The distinction between psychological recognition of guilt-feeling and its cure, and the Christian concept of sin, penitence, and absolution, cannot here be explored, but the theatre today is

35

concerned with these matters. The secular playwrights struggle to find a rational, daylight solution to the dark tensions of the spirit of man. In Act II of *Godot* the tramps wait before the return of Pozzo and Lucky. They are waiting for the Saviour. When none comes, they begin to imitate the ritual of Lucky. They "do the tree." They want communal activity, and they want a channel for emotion. In Greene's play, set as it is severely within the Roman Catholic framework, the existence of such rituals is implicit in what the audience knows about the Roman Church. But a part of the priest James's crippled condition is that he has been for years unable to perform the rituals. He is lamed thereby, as much as by his paralysis.

Those who, like some secular humanists, attempt to discount man's irrationality, also discount his need for ritual. This attempt has repercussions upon the drama, for (as Aristotle saw) drama, if powerful and true, performs for its participants a religious purgation; it achieves this end through participation in ritual. A need for ritual connotes irrationality and weakness. It demands that irrational and weak human beings acknowledge that they cannot live fully without external help, and that this help can be mediated through religious rites. To the humanist, this may well seem all nonsense—away with it! And with the nonsense, away goes the poetry, away goes the power, and the glory, and knowledge of the redemptive grace of God, and away also go the unresolved anxiety-states and the creative tensions out of which much drama grows.

2
HOW WE
GOT THERE

Before the New Theatre

It is no part of this study to attempt to trace the emergence of drama from its earliest religious origins, whether Memphite or Greek, through mystery and morality plays, the Puritan ban, and so on, to January 5, 1953. That is the domain of scholars. What concerns us is to mark the points of contact between theatre and church as they emerge in the last few years and to draw what conclusions we can from such observations. To do this will, however, necessitate a rapid glance at the recent past. We begin with three dramatists who handled religious themes in the "old" theatre: Ibsen, Shaw, and Claudel.

Ibsen in 1866, no less than Goethe in 1806, was committed to a battle against falsity wherever he detected it. The Enlightenment bequeathed this legacy: he had to accept it. For our discussion, Ibsen's first play, *Brand*,[1] is probably his most important, with its story of the righteous man, the pastor Brand, who obeys the law to the last execution of the letter, and sacrifices his entire circle—mother, wife, child, friends, and in the end his own life—to his own image of virtue, to a God of his own creation who delights only in broken hearts and victims offered upon altars of stone.

---

[1] Different translations are available from Doubleday & Company (Anchor Books, ed.); E. P. Dutton & Co. (Everyman's Library, ed.); and Theatre Arts.

One can learn from the intensity of this play, from its fierce drive to find the answer to Brand's need for God, something of the burden placed upon a sensitive and truthful spirit by the negativism of the church life of Ibsen's environment. One can understand and sympathize with the dramatist's anger against society's acceptance of this negativism, an anger more violent than that unleashed against any of the manifestations of social dishonesty which Ibsen attacks in his other plays.

"Rage, rage, against the dying of the light!" Ibsen truly rages, with full as much force as Dylan Thomas, against any situation which, in his view, quenches or dims the light of truth. Yet, while he rages, he learns. And we may learn. We observe evil in society first; but, as understanding deepens, we are compelled to recognize that, for real achievement, the writer himself

> Must lie down where all the ladders start,
> In the foul rag-and-bone-shop of the heart.[2]

Ibsen dared, with increasing mastery of his medium, to use the theatre as a place where rage against dishonesty of any kind could find a voice, and where the worst condemnation was that reserved for those who chose darkness rather than light.

The appeal of his passion for truth made Ibsen the hero, idol, and model of the next great figure of the theatre's immediate past—George Bernard Shaw. Shaw's contribu-

[2] Reprinted with permission of The Macmillan Company from "The Circus Animal's Desertion," by W. B. Yeats. Copyright 1940 by Georgie Yeats.

tion to our current theatre is for the moment undervalued, though without his rebellious wit and the fifty-two plays in which he demonstrated it, the public for serious theatre would have been sadly undernourished in the first thirty years of this century. To the reader or playgoer who comes new to him today, he may seem both long-winded and complacent. Master of prose though he is, his certainties have been outpaced by events. He may indeed seem to be slightly more in touch with scientific thought than the rest of his immediate contemporaries: for example, Lilith's last speech in *Back to Methuselah* (1925) seems to take into account something of modern astronomical discovery. But that speech itself is written out of an assurance few could command today. "Of life only there is no end: and though of its million starry mansions many are empty and many still unbuilt . . . my seed shall one day fill it and master its matter to its uttermost confines. And for what may be beyond, the eyesight of Lilith is too short. It is enough that there *is* a Beyond." The most confident humanist would hesitate today before penning such a curtainline; and no chair of "Metabiology" has yet been founded in any of our new universities.

For our purposes the two of Shaw's plays which are most relevant, apart from *Back to Methuselah,* are *Androcles and the Lion* (1915) and *Too True to Be Good,* written for the Malvern Festival 1932.[3] In the long preface to *Androcles,* as in the play itself, Shaw presents a criticism of the church as he saw it, quite as discouraging as that deducible from Ibsen's *Brand.* He accuses us of being what

[3] *Complete Plays with Prefaces,* Vol. IV (New York: Dodd, Mead and Company).

he called "Iconolaters," worshipers of a "fixed and static image of Christ," and he warns us "the moment it strikes you . . . that Christ is not the lifeless, harmless image he has hitherto been to you, but a rallying centre for revolutionary influence which all established states and churches fight, you must look to yourselves: for you will have brought the image to life: and the mob cannot bear that horror. . . . But mobs must be faced if civilization is to be saved." Fair enough, and not only in 1915. But, in practice, what does Shaw propose? During the intervening twenty years between the two plays, he moved from the attack on the weakness of the church as it failed to grapple with the new science of his period, to the sad late cadences as he faced not only the breakdown of the idea of inevitable evolutionary progress in an upward direction, but also the chanciness of the universe, the apparent lack of precisely that stable natural law upon which the young Shaw had so confidently counted. He sees instead a reeling world—"We are all like drunken women clinging to lamp posts"—and to end a play which begins with the question "What does the Lord require of a man but to do justice and love mercy and walk humbly with his God?" all that Shaw can find is the despairing question of Aubrey as he stands in the fading light: "Is No enough? For a boy, yes; for a man, never!" And he concludes, inconclusively: "And I must go on preaching, no matter how late the hour, no matter how short the day, no matter whether I have nothing to say."

In Ibsen, violent reaction from the negative prohibitions of too stern a protestantism; in Shaw, despairing endurance of the death-throes of liberalism. We see two men both critical of the *status quo ante,* neither didactic in the strict sense of the word. But Paul Claudel, the Frenchman, was not ashamed to preach. Though a cradle-Catholic, he grew up in a society dominated, as was Shaw's, by the doctrine of evolutionary progress. He was more and more unhappy in this rationalist environment until, in 1890, he returned to the church of his baptism. Shaw, traveling in Europe four years later, noted: "Religion was alive again, coming back upon men, even clergymen, with such power that not the Church of England itself could keep it out." It may well have seemed that Claudel's regained faith was but one sign of this alleged religious revival. What is certain is that Claudel's work introduces into the drama an element long absent. He speaks of *grace*. Perhaps for the first time on any stage since *Macbeth, Winter's Tale*, and *Measure for Measure* were presented, the necessity for "grace to live well" was stated in the play *L'annonce faite à Marie*.[4] It was stated in a cool fluid verse stanza of Claudel's own contriving, which was to contribute much to the communication possible to the theatre. We are here far from Shaw's early belief that, given time, man could save himself by his own effort and others by his own pugnacity. In Claudel's great play, Christian dogma influences the form, and Christian terminology the expression, of a play which is set indeed in the Middle Ages, but which tells the universal story of human rebellion from, and human submission to, the overruling will of a God manifest to humanity.

The play took many years to complete before its first production in 1912, and the melodrama of the plot, if summarized, gives as little indication of the play's quality as

[4] Edited by A. L. Sells and C. M. Girdlestone (London: Cambridge University Press, 1943).

would a synopsis of Goethe's *Faust*. It is uniquely successful in its linking of the simultaneous cruelty and loveliness of the natural world to the miraculously redemptive quality of total human response to the penetration of the spirit, of total self-surrender to the demand of divine love.

That Claudel, as dramatist, was formed upon the Greek classical theatre is a matter of importance, as it is a matter of regret that Shaw never underwent such a discipline. Claudel, by his studies of the classics, was educated to accept the myth, the symbolic statement of a given culture, as the prime source of drama. His imagination and understanding were, from the same source, nourished, throughout his period of youthful atheism, upon a religious view of life. His apprenticeship to the drama was served by translating the *Agamemnon, Choephoroe,* and *Eumenides;* when he began his original work for the theatre it was with the avowed didactic intention of presenting, upon the French stage, themes which have always preoccupied religious minds—the inscrutable justice of heaven, the moral reality of hell, and the extent of human responsibility for human error. These are Greek themes, and Claudel linked with them the specifically Christian doctrines (no doubt of particular importance to him in the reawakening of his own faith) of grace, of penitence and of vicarious atonement—subjects indeed alien to the theatre of the early twentieth century, whether French or English.

We turn briefly now to the serious drama of Europe and England in the 1920s and '30s. Defeat, revolution, and poverty called for a quite different kind of recreation from that offered by the prewar theatre. The experimental

42

theatre voiced the new mood. Like Elmer Rice's *Adding Machine* in the USA, in Czechoslovakia the Capek brothers' *Insect Play* showed men as creatures without dignity—the ant and the mayfly. The general impression was that "An End" was about the best that man can hope for. In *Masses and Men,* a play of immense force, violent and morbid, the German Communist leader, Ernst Toller, showed humanity laden with inexpiable guilt.

The wheel revolves; and it is an urgent question for our social psychologists to investigate, whether there is not a certain kind of temperament which, rejecting formal religion and the safeguards to be found in tested ritual, seeks to propitiate its own Eumenides by a communal ritual experience. This goes far deeper than the Protestant/Catholic emphasis. The impact on Germany of *Masses and Men* after World War I—like the powerful effect in Berlin of *The Diary of Anne Frank* after World War II, or even the impressively staged public trial of Eichmann in Israel in 1962—was linked with the human need for an externalizing of guilt-feeling, the need for an expiatory rite.

The serious plays of postwar Europe in the Twenties were shown in settings of black or grey curtains, or of stepped bare stages with light used symbolically, eschewing any attempt at naturalism. We are sometimes told today that the current bare-stage fashion is due to a desire to focus all interest on the individual human being, freeing him from locality, history, class, or even gender. This was not the aim of the Twenties. The actors made direct address to the audience, and the whole objective was that actors and audience should share together an experience of mass-exaltation and mass-purgation.

The great experimental producer of the 1920 period, Max Reinhardt, used the circus theatre (theatre in the round or arena theatre as we should now call it) in an effort to identify spectator with spectacle. Reinhardt wanted to use what he called the "Theatre of the Five Thousand" to express and release what he described as "emotions simple and primitive, but great and powerful as becomes the eternal human race." He could hardly know it, but the arch-producer, Adolf Hitler, was in the wings. Max Reinhardt was helping to prepare his people for the Nuremberg rallies and the appalling mob-response to mob-stimuli.

In England there was not the same ardor to experiment in the theatre—and there was no Nuremberg rally. But we had the same desire to produce plays which should speak to the postwar Englishman's condition. Admittedly the postwar Englishman was for the most part fairly happy with the five-year run of the musical *Chu-Chin-Chow* which fed his starved senses with movement and color and a sugared exoticism. But the serious theatre now profited by the unbroken stream of poetic dramatists who had continued to experiment (at the Abbey Theatre, Dublin, one or two provincial Repertories, notably Liverpool and Birmingham, and the London little theatres) with ideas and forms of dramatic expression that had little to do with the continental development. Two such plays were Yeats's *Countess Cathleen* and Synge's *Riders to the Sea*.

W. B. Yeats's *Countess Cathleen*,[5] written in 1892 but produced only very tentatively and infrequently till after 1918, shows the divine compassion as exemplified in the

[5] In his *Collected Plays* (New York: The Macmillan Company, 1953).

44

Countess who (Faust-like but with a difference) makes a bargain with the Devil, giving her soul, not for temporal joys for herself, but for bread for her starving peasants. J. M. Synge's *Riders to the Sea*,[6] set on the coast of Ireland, shows an old woman from whom everything is gradually taken away, and brings the symbolism of the Eucharist into the daily tragedy of the seafarer's hovel.

Here we see two writers of extreme sensibility presenting to us the turning point in a soul's development—the Countess Cathleen's willed suffering of death for her people, the peasant Maury's resignation of her personal anguish into the hands of a God felt rather than known to be at once more merciful and sterner than man can understand. Yet the God of both these plays is a God in a remote heaven—remote whether in time or space. "Art thou he that should come, or do we look for another?" All through this period right up to World War II (Masefield, Galsworthy, Shaw, Drinkwater, Gordon Bottomley, even the early Auden), we find this question "Art thou he?" being posed. Where is the answer, for Man? Is it in the social revolution? In worker's solidarity? Does it lie in self-abnegation, or in the human determination to eat of the tree of life? Does it consist just in being kindly to one another? Or does it reside in J. M. Barrie's land of fairy whimsy?

At length, in 1928, something happened which was a turning point. At Canterbury (Bishop George Bell being then Dean of the Cathedral) the first of the Canterbury Cathedral plays was produced—John Masefield's *Coming*

[6] In his *Complete Plays* (New York: Vintage Books, 1960).

of Christ.[7] A group of interested people found a focus where they could make use, for play production in church, of the techniques with which Reinhardt had been experimenting (he had already produced Calderon's *Great Theatre of the World*). They made use of the verse forms which had been forged by the poetic dramatists, and of enthusiastic support from a handful of faithful church men and women. In Christian terminology, but in tune with the current mood which was still very far from today's negativism, Masefield's play expressed the overwhelming sense of man's eternal need of a saviour. It was as though the remorseless voice of the summoning of Everyman [8] to face death, given full and horrifying reality in the events of the war of 1914-18 and its ghastly aftermath, had been echoing and reechoing in the windy corridors of our history, until twenty years later the theme was taken up again in a poet's presentation of a Coming which had to take place because men knew at last that they had no power of themselves to help themselves and were, as they are not today, prepared to believe that help *could* come from outside themselves. In the performing of such a play in such a place, a relation was at last established between church and theatre.

In 1935, again in Canterbury Cathedral, listeners to another poetic drama heard the words:

Here let us stand, close by the Cathedral. Here let us wait.
Are we drawn by danger? Is it the knowledge of safety that draws
Our feet towards the Cathedral? . . .

[7] (London: William Heinemann Ltd., 1928.)
[8] The play *Everyman* was produced by William Peel in 1909.

Some presage of an act
Which our eyes are compelled to witness has forced our feet
Towards the Cathedral. We are forced to bear witness.

To many of us in that dark and uneasy period between Hitler's rise to power and the outbreak of war in 1939, T. S. Eliot's *Murder in the Cathedral* [9] had a power quite beyond the literary merit which later generations may detect in it. He spoke of the "presage of an act." The act was the betrayal first of Europe and then of the world's humanity, a betrayal of which we had had clear warning.

I have consented, Lord Archbishop, have consented.
Am torn away, subdued, violated . . .

Dominated by the lust of self-demolition. . . .

Dust I am, to dust am bending,
From the final doom impending
Help me, Lord, for death is near.

It was the mood of the *Dies Irae*. But what has time to do with judgment? No one since Shakespeare had thought fit to explore the relativity of time in terms of the theatre, though phrases from the mathematicians' studies were beginning to filter into popular writing. J. B. Priestley, ever with a flair for the moment, sensed the importance of the new ways of thinking of time as they affected men's apprehension of judgment, and he was attracted by Ouspensky's theory of the possibility of spirals in human experi-

[9] (Harcourt, Brace & World [1935].)

ence. Out of this material he produced his "time plays," in particular his *I Have Been Here Before*.[10] This play shows a married couple who have reached the parting of their ways and who are led to a new level of being by the fact that the husband, helped by a mysterious German philosopher, takes the leap upwards to the next level of being by his refusal to commit suicide. By his willed rejection of death for himself, he releases all those connected with his life to start a new series of relationships, each better, in the sense of being nearer to eternal life, than any relationship they have previously been able to attain.

Few Christians seized upon this tentative approach of the secular theatre to such a problem as Priestley's. The gap between theatre and church was too wide for our lazy minds to attempt to bridge it or to relate the new ideas to Christian doctrine; and so we see an unfortunate situation developing. Those who feared went with Eliot into the cathedral; those who *dared* moved further and further away from what Christians regard as the real sources of "eternal life." *Murder in the Cathedral,* while making church plays respectable for church people, was, some think, a false move because it tended to make church people concentrate on "plays suitable for churches" while the true life-giving line should really have been to find and foster the secular dramatists in the theatre and discover means to show them how and where what they were doing related to the structure of the Christian faith, and to integrate the drama ever more closely with *popular* life. T. S. Eliot, of course, was himself far too sage to remain underneath the arches; his subsequent plays were for the secular

[10] Now in the Essential English Library, Longmans.

theatre. But we have still not achieved an integration, or even a creative dialogue, between theatre and church.[11]

It is saddening to think what opportunities have been lost. Christian theologians are not yet accustomed to devote much time to discussion with playwrights as they grapple with the mystery of the human spirit's nature. Yet they are greatly needed here. It is possible to conceive of great music, as of mathematics, existing in a world where sequence, order, balance, were predictable and stable, where permutations and combinations, even risk, though theoretically infinite, could be computed, controlled, manipulated. Ballet might exist in such a world, so might abstract painting, so might architecture. But the drama? Is drama possible without mystery? What does it mean when *order*, "degree," is shattered? This question inflames the imagination of a great playwright, because it brings to full consciousness our ignorance about Being, our *un*predictability, our *ir*rationality and, for the Christian, our need for God's grace. Without an acceptance of this "burden of the mystery" the serious theatre must inevitably decline. Neither proscenium arch nor theatre-in-the-round can save a drama that evades the ultimate questions. And a church that is not in touch with its contemporary theatre is a church neglecting one of the channels of grace. The struggle of drama, in its own measure the same as the struggle of faith, is to become, and remain, interwoven with the life of the common man.

[11] The problems were discussed by Robert Speaight, who played the part of the Archbishop in *Murder in the Cathedral,* in *The Christian Theatre,* Burns and Oates, 1961.

3

TO SAY NO,
AND DIE

Three Plays About Integrity

It is evident that in the theatre of Beckett—in the secular "new" theatre—there can be no glib statement of the Christian view of the human condition. But something can be said. We now turn to study three contemporary plays which stand on the frontier between (what to a Christian is) faith and (what to a Christian is) unbelief. They are plays about the integrity or honor of a modern person, and about the possibility or impossibility today of a total commitment. They are *Antigone* by Jean Anouilh, *Les Justes* by Albert Camus, and *Marching Song* by John Whiting.

First, *Antigone*.[1] Antigone, niece of Creon the King, is engaged to Haemon, Creon's Son. Antigone and her sister, Ismene, had two brothers, Eteocles and Polynices, who inherited the throne between them, each to reign over Thebes in alternate years. The two brothers fought, and killed each other in single combat just outside the city walls. Now that Creon is king he has issued a solemn edict that Eteocles, with whom he had sided, is to be buried with pomp and honors, and that Polynices is to be left to rot. Any person who attempts to give him religious burial will himself be put to death.

Anouilh's play was first performed in Paris on February

[1] Copyright by La Table Ronde.

4, 1944. It was designed to be acted to an audience for whom the question of commitment was no theoretical question. In France throughout World War II, the theatre was one of the focal points of the resistance movement. The first audience of this play knew full well what it meant to have to decide not only what was theoretically right to do, but to do it, often at the cost of life. In Paris in World War II during the German occupation the playwright could indeed count upon an audience capable of giving him full participation in shared assumptions. Of course it would have been impossible to stage a play which dealt directly with the subject of resistance in World War II. It was wiser to distance the play's message if you wanted to avoid trouble. So the choice of Antigone's story was one for which the reason is obvious. And how beautifully Anouilh plants his argument! Ismene, Antigone's sister, expresses all the collaborationist ideals, and expresses them with perfect theatrical tact and naturalness.

> *Ismene:* I think things out.
> *Antigone:* The howling mob, the torture, the fear of death; they've made up your mind for you, is that it?
> *Ismene:* Yes.
> *Antigone:* All right. They're as good excuses as any.

Antigone makes her point, the point of many a martyrdom, when she tells the tyrant Creon: "I am not here to understand. I am here to say no, and die."

There follows the wonderful scene between Creon and Antigone on the subject of happiness. Creon thinks he is succeeding in persuading Antigone to recant and save herself and "be happy." Antigone refuses:

51

Now it is you who have stopped understanding. I am too far away from you now, talking to you from a kingdom you can't get into, with your quick tongue and your hollow heart.

She dies, of course. So does Haemon, so does Creon's wife Eurydice. Creon is left with the characteristic words of the man who has sold his soul and does not like what he has got in exchange. "They don't know it, but the truth is there is work to be done, and a man can't fold his arms and refuse to do it. They say it's dirty work. But if we didn't do it, who would?"

And the chorus speaks the final word:

All those who were meant to die have died; those who believed one thing, those who believed the contrary thing, and even those who believed nothing at all, yet were caught up in the web without knowing why. All dead: stiff, useless, rotting. It is all over. Antigone is calm tonight and we shall never know the name of the fever that consumed her.

A thoughtful Christian will note the connection between this and the movement of tragedy in John's Gospel. The sacrificial victim, the Lamb, whose feet do not need to be washed, tries to explain to the betrayer Creon what it means to reject happiness for honor. "Honor" is a word which has become cheapened in daily use. But it still has some of the connotations of the scriptural "glory." Indeed, *la gloire* and *l'honneur* are two central terms in the forming of the *honnête homme,* the full man—the "whole person" as we now say. All these points affect Antigone's reasons for willing herself to a hideous death. But Creon the Betrayer cannot understand. Antigone is in a kingdom which he cannot enter. Has Antigone then moved into the dimension of life eternal? No. And here is the difference. Antigone's act has relevance only in so far as it affects her nation, her city, her *polis*. It is in the highest sense of the term a political martyrdom. It is also an excellent example of existential drama. The exploration is an exploration of the self, but the self, in Anouilh's play, is the sum total of its acts.

One of the cruelties of our situation today is the powerlessness of individual action. Even young children experience this powerlessness in a new way. The definition which Kierkegaard gives of the "alienation" experienced spiritually by our age is also a description of what France and other occupied countries experienced politically no less than philosophically, namely: the experience of being in a state of anxiety, dominated by an alien power which threatens our dissolution, when we cannot save ourselves by our own acts. In spite of the fact that his heroine's sacrifice effects nothing *practically*, yet Anouilh is putting to us the same question that Kierkegaard puts, namely: Can the fatal leveling process of our time be stopped by the courage and dauntlessness of persons accepting an absolute responsibility?

Anouilh speaks of absolutes, and so in part disguises from us, perhaps, the gulf between existentialist drama and the Christian standpoint. The gulf is clearer in another play of commitment, *Les Justes*, translated as *The Just Assassins*,[2] by Albert Camus. Here the protagonists are revolutionaries committed to the assassination of a tyrant grand duke. In a

[2] E. O. Marsh (ed.) (London: George G. Harrap & Co., 1960.)

53

skillful intertwining of human hate and love, Camus shows us nothing but the white heat to which human loyalty can be fired—and the price that human beings are ready and able to pay in order to stand by a personal commitment. It is this dauntlessness for an absolute that gives universal importance to the *Antigone* theme, and it is of prime importance that Christians should know where they stand in this question; not necessarily to know what is the "right" answer but what answer any one of us is ready to bet our lives on.

One looks to Brecht, perhaps in *Mother Courage*, but Brecht has no answer.[3] For him there is no such entity as peace; there is only existence or nonexistence. Anouilh, in *Antigone*, regards hope as a hideous deception. Peace and strength are found only in acceptance of human helplessness. The acceptance can be heroic: It is not Christian.

Where the story of Christ's passion moves in a different sphere from that of the sacrifice of Antigone is that, as John tells the story, the responsibility is Godward and God participates both as agent and as victim. In *Antigone* the effect of her action, as has been shown, is purely political. Antigone's task is to be herself, because hers is an absolute commitment the reverse of expediency, demanded of her for her *polis*, because the *polis* has suffered through the expedient government of Creon. The task of the Lord is other; it is to draw all men. The commitment is equal; the penalty, humanly speaking, the same. But the *stakes* are not comparable. Antigone's death will not turn the world upside down.

[3] See J. Willet, *The Theatre of Bertolt Brecht* (New York: New Directions, 1959).

Camus' play is intensely gripping and yet, at the end, one lacks the sense of purgation and the resultant peace which one experiences in the true classical tragedy. Why is this? Is the Christian who sees *Les Justes* unsatisfied because Christian presuppositions demand, for their satisfaction, more than can be offered by a stoic humanist such as Camus? Or is the play itself unsatisfactory because in fact it is a doctrinaire piece, which at some point hard to detect *cheats* in its own mode, and in purely dramatic terms dodges the resolution implicit in the theme? In discussing the weaknesses of Graham Greene's play, it appeared that Greene had not succeeded in establishing a mode of expressing *through action* the word he wished to speak to his audience, and so preached, instead of communicating in the true dramatic mode. Is this the case with *Les Justes?*

Jacques Guicharnaud has some light to throw on our difficulty. He says of Camus: "All his works are dominated by intellectual searching and the examination of ideas. Yet what distinguishes his plays from other philosophical theatre is the dramatic and concrete nature of the philosophy itself. The fundamental problem of the definition of man and the world is truly embodied in living *acts*." [4] Quite so. And perhaps unease springs exactly from this "embodiment." For Christians hold that no man is *only* the sum of his acts. From examining an unease, therefore, it appears that it is a religious difficulty which prevents one's acceptance of the end of *Les Justes*. At the end of Sophocles' *Oedipus,* though Oedipus is innocent and yet doomed, one feels total acceptance of the situation. For with a piercing

[4] *Modern French Theatre,* p. 151.

clarity like that which blinds the tyrant king, or like that which causes Beckett's Pozzo to know himself blind, Sophocles shows that there is *mystery* in destiny: that man is not merely the sum of his acts, but one link in a spiritual chain. And this is denied by the existential drama.

John Whiting's untimely death has deprived the English stage of one of its most promising hopes. In his play *Marching Song* [5] he examines the same situation as is found in *Les Justes*. *Marching Song* is set in a city which after war has fallen under a dictatorship. Catherine de Troyes, a foreigner settled in the city during the war, is supported by an odd crowd of hangers-on who are somehow necessary to her own spiritual survival. The play deals with the return, from imprisonment in a camp in the mountains, of the hero, Rupert Forster, Catherine's lover. The action hinges upon the change effected in the hero by what he has been through, both in the appalling mode of warfare to which he was forced in a crucial battle, and subsequently in his experience of military disgrace and solitary confinement. While he has been absent, Catherine, surrounding herself by what would preserve in her circumstances the *status quo ante,* has lost touch with him. And he is supported, as he makes his choice between life and death, not by Catherine, but by a girl of the back streets, a vagrant, a drifter, who has nevertheless anchored her soul to the need to accept, to be in the moment—to be (like Antigone only not in the face of peril) herself. The line which Whiting chose to place on the flyleaf of the published play is "Well, honour

[5] © John Whiting 1953. Whiting's complete *Plays* are published by William Heinemann, Ltd.

is the subject of my story." The hero's final decision is the old formula, banal if you like, "Death rather than dishonour." There is a kind of God-figure in the form of the dictator, John Cadmus, with whom Catherine, during Forster's absence, has developed an ambiguous relationship.

The setting is one large upstairs room of stone, glass, and steel warmed by fabrics and furnishings—at one side there is a plinth surmounted by an antique bronze helmet still containing the skull which was in it when it was dug up. The first words are spoken by an American film cameraman, a hanger-on of Catherine de Troyes, one Harry Lancaster, a once successful filmmaker, now finished, though he will not admit it. He has brought with him a girl who will (he pretends to himself) *make* his next film. The girl, Dido Morgen, is hungry, a waif of the city. But she is honest. She wants to know about this Catherine, who she is, and whether she has money. She notices the helmet and inquires about it. Harry tells her it belonged to Rupert Forster, who lived here with Catherine but is now imprisoned because, says Harry, he "went beyond the limits the world will tolerate." Forster and Catherine, he says, were "beautiful." So was the world. "In the old days?" queries Dido mockingly. Dido doesn't interest herself one jot in looking backward. Catherine, who now appears, is in this respect her opposite. With Catherine come Father Anselm and Doctor Langosse, ministers to a soul and body in a *fixed* condition. When Rupert went away, Catherine says later in the play, she could neither pray nor sleep. Hence these two, who take over those sides of life for her, safeguarding her from the necessity for any fundamental change in her *self*. Harry introduces Dido, and Catherine says she may stay the night, but tells both that the game is over, for Forster has returned to her. In fact, Forster has been allowed to return from prison but only under guard. John Cadmus, the dictator of the city, intends to use Forster as a scapegoat. Harry, with his professional's eye for drama, spots a resemblance to Shakespeare's *Coriolanus*. "If you listen very hard," he says, "you'll hear the sounds of war. 'Coriolan—Coriolan.' You'll hear the soft stumbling tread of returning men, men out of order and out of heart. There's no drum can fit the broken rhythm of their march."

Here Rupert himself enters and points out that in fact he and Coriolanus are *un*like, because Coriolanus was a tyrant where he, Rupert, is a soldier under discipline. Rupert asks about the hangers-on and Catherine explains. Forster tells her what his life in prison was: the utter deprivation of everything which had previously nourished him, a deprivation into which he willingly entered, refusing fantasy, indulgence, or any amelioration of his lot. He does not at this point say why he did this. At present he just wants Catherine to put aside any idea that the old life can be resumed between them.

Harry Lancaster and Rupert then discuss the right use of power, and the discussion preludes the entry of John Cadmus, who is described as "physically and spiritually wasted by many years spent in the exercise of power"—"A father-image, Daddy Cadmus, they call me," he says of himself. And, now, strangely, Daddy Cadmus explains that it is expedient that one man should die for the people. There must be a sin-eater, a scapegoat. People *need* to say "I wasn't guilty," and the only way they can be sure of this is if they can add "He was." Cadmus gives Forster a box of poison. Rupert takes the box. Catherine cries "He is safe with me," and Cadmus replies: "Any complete protection is also a prison." Catherine and Rupert are left alone and Rupert tells Catherine the truth—that he no longer loves her, and that he will no longer lie to anyone.

At this moment they are joined by Dido Morgen, whose name, as she herself tells us, "matters." Dido is the catalyst in this play. She causes change in others. Dido, the Carthaginian queen, was fatally ensnared by love of a warrior on his way home, and on his departure flung herself upon a funeral pyre and was consumed to ashes. Not so Dido Morgen! This Dido is for the morrow. She fully intends to keep herself free for that future. This is *her* commitment, as a triumph of arms was Rupert's, and as the preserving of the *status quo ante* was Catherine's.

Rupert Forster has already taken several steps toward this readiness, but it is the advent of Dido, her calm openness towards the future, and her refusal to repine over the past, which helps him to make the final act of resolve. In this struggle Catherine is no use to him. She wants to keep him safe. But Dido wants freedom for him. She asks him why he never married. He kept his freedom from the marriage commitment in order the more fully to honor his commitment as soldier. Dido's freedom stems from a different cause. She is aware of her own weakness. "I am not strong enough, or wise enough to have another living, loving person with me." She sees through the traps set by kindness; she has been caught by kindness before. Now she intends to keep clear. Rupert says you can keep free if you have an objective. His objective in fighting was to

59

impose himself. "Saints need a religion. I had to pursue a triumph of arms." And he has no sooner made this statement than he disproves it. In the big speech of the play, he shows us that the turning point in his life was the moment when the achieved objective itself proved suddenly to bring with it the destruction of his freedom.

He describes the moment when he was about to order his tank force into action in what appeared to be a deserted village.

A little boy had come from the church and was standing on the steps. He put his hand to his mouth—oh, as if to put in a sweet—but it was a whistle he held. He blew the whistle and at once the children were upon us, hundreds of them. They came from the church, from the houses on the street, and from far off down the street itself. They rolled like a wave towards us, screaming and shouting, some armed with sticks, some carrying flags. Reaching us they beat themselves against the sides of our tanks. I saw my commanders and their crews laughing at them. We might have been liberators not an attacking force. *Was I the only man to see the danger?* We were virtually immobilized, for they were everywhere, even beneath the tracks. The laughter of my men became louder—our concentration was broken. The attack, timed by seconds to coordination, was flinging itself to pieces. My central armoured force was the governing factor of the movement; delay it and the two infantry groups became as ineffective as naked men. The boy who had come first from the church had clambered on my tank. He was black-haired and black-eyed and he carried a wooden sword which he swung above his head. He shouted something I didn't understand and then spat at me. *That* was no provocation for what I did. I had already decided. I stretched out and drew his head to my shoulder like a lover, and shot him in the mouth. I took him by the hair of his shattered head and held him up for my men to see. They understood. The shooting began . . . and we moved forward.

Dido: They say four hundred were found dead.
Rupert: Do they? I had no idea.
Dido: What was the place?
Rupert: A children's colony, I was told later. They were of all nationalities—some of the enemy, some of our own, herded together by the shuttle of armies. Nobody's discovered what they were about that morning. Reckless imitation of their fathers and brothers? Put up to it by unscrupulous commanders? Or had those children reached a point from which there is no further retreat and a *stand* —against whatever odds—must at last be made?

It is the same situation as that in *Antigone*—the situation, in the last analysis, of every martyrdom. There comes a point from which there is no further retreat, and a stand must be made.

Cadmus, on his return to hear Rupert's decision, at once senses the danger to his plans that Dido represents. Dido's support has changed Rupert; he can now make a willed choice, not a compulsive one.

The two discuss the nature of freedom and of what makes men continue to live. Rupert says:

A man is an army, a striking offensive force. Each of us has a line of communication stretching out. The line goes back to other people, places, ideas. From you and Catherine back into the past, from myself and the girl out to the immediate

61

happening. But we all call it by the same name, don't we, Cadmus? Love. And as long as that line remains open, we have to live.

Cadmus takes occasion to show Rupert clearly what disgrace will do to him. There is a horrible moment when Lancaster cannot refrain from an expression of pleasure that Rupert will be at last "brought down to our level"— the perennial envy and hate common men feel for the hero. Dido and Rupert are left together. Rupert sleeps and Dido Morgen keeps the morning watch.

Act II shows Rupert left alone with Cadmus and Bruno, a young captain of the guard. Rupert has been a hero of the young Bruno and Bruno asks him, as a matter of technical interest, *why* he delayed his advance after the shooting of the children. Rupert says:

> I couldn't free myself from that moment, the moment when I stood alone, sad, lost, childless, with the child in my arms. And looking down saw that it was a human being. It was then the secret was forced upon me. I'd shut it out until that morning by making my own prison years before they sent me to the camp in the mountains— a prison of pride and ambition. Then when I caught the child to me, the secret was revealed. I suddenly understood what a man is. For I held it close.
>
> *Bruno:* If you felt this, why did you shoot?
> *Rupert:* I had no choice. The way I'd chosen to live led to that encounter.
> *Bruno:* You must consider yourself guilty.
> *Rupert:* I do.

Well, Rupert takes the poison and dies. Cadmus knew that he would. "I knew him as a man very much like myself. But he'd something I've had to put away whilst I'm in office. *Honour.* So I knew what the end would be." "Are you telling me that you also suffer in this?" "I suppose, in a way, I am."

The play ends with a wonderful quietness and simplicity, the effect of which is totally different from the equally quiet ending of *Antigone.* In *Marching Song,* one has the feeling that a purgation has been effected, all the pain exhibited for our learning has meaning. Rupert, long committed to establishing an honor, a reputation, which brings and can only bring death, *changes* his commitment. And the change is total. If openness to the future is a mark of faith, then this is a faithful play. Moreover, Rupert's acceptance of death does release others for the future too. Harry Lancaster, the drunken shadow-man, becomes aware of his filthiness. Catherine de Troyes becomes aware of her coldness. The last word is with Dido, who had left the scene to regain her own free world, but who returns, right at the end, to where Catherine and Harry are still on stage. She moves towards Catherine and, speaking the last line of the play, says with a shy delicacy of dedication: "Catherine—what I know—can it be taught? I'll try."

Compare this lovely *open* ending with the closed doom of the Nazi family, the Gerlachs, in Sartre's *The Condemned of Altona,*[6] and you gain some notion of the Christian as against the non-Christian view of life.

There remains the question of structure as related to belief. These two plays by Anouilh and Whiting are examples of plays where the belief is integrated with the

[6] (New York: Alfred A. Knopf, 1961.)

action and where the action springs directly out of the characters. And Anouilh is here far the better technician of the two.

In *Antigone* as in *Marching Song,* the crucial act has already been performed when the play opens. The heroine is already doomed. Justice has only to take its course. Antigone is youth personified, responsive to every natural perfection. Ismene, her sister, tempts Antigone to recant. She resists. Nurse tempts her. She resists. Haemon, her lover, tempts her. She resists. The whole ebb and flow of each brief scene carries the action further, the final crashing wave brings the revelation we have been holding our breath to receive. "You are too late, Ismene. When you first saw me this morning I had just come in from burying Poly- nices." The irony in which we have participated has thrown into clear relief the character of Antigone. It recalls Yeats's definition of drama as "character isolated by a deed."

For classical tragedy the plot must be limited to the length of time necessary to show the effects of the deed, the crucial action. If the crucial action is Antigone's burial of Polynices, what are the effects? First, Antigone's own death; and we have seen how she resists the temptation to evade this. The second effect is that upon Creon, and Anouilh in the second scene deals with the discussion between Creon and Antigone. Creon tempts her, but she resists him too, and we are reminded of the trial of Jesus, in that it is the purity of the victim by which the judge him- self is condemned. Creon fails to win Antigone, and, im- mediately after, fails also to win his own son, Haemon. Antigone has then to undergo death and we have to be shown the effect of this death upon the other actors in the tragedy. Haemon dies too, rather than live without her. Eurydice, the queen, dies rather than live without Haemon, her son. The only one who remains unmoved is Creon, for he exists in a different dimension. He is concerned only with *acts*, not with relationships at all.

So the play's structure is sound. It follows logically the necessities of destiny and takes only the time necessary for us to see the effect of the crucial action on the chief performers.

No character in *Antigone* has changed one iota from what it was when the play began. This is classically correct —it is also consistent with the French existentialist position, that all man can be concerned with is his own integrity. Nothing in the plot leads Antigone away from her concern with her own integrity, nor does anything develop in Creon which might redeem him from the doom his complacency has made for him. It is perfectly clear that Antigone has accepted, in accepting the duty of burying Polynices, a duty which overrides every other consideration. She is not sacrificing herself for another human being or for any god. The Christian attitude is: "I do not so much choose as submit to being chosen for this duty." There is nothing of this in Antigone. Her choice is her own. And it it raised to heroic power by the purity of her acceptance of the consequences of her choice. In order to show this purity of acceptance in Antigone at full blaze, so to speak, Anouilh allows us to follow through her purgation (the purification of the sacrifice, if you like to think of it so) until we feel sure that she is now wholly dedicated, her character wholly subordinated to the act she must *become*. There are parallels to the Gethsemane story all through, not only in the use of the garden introduction. The silent victim, the anxious political judge already condemned by his inability to understand the victim at all, the apparent uselessness of the gesture of sacrifice, the secret entombment, the mother's heart also pierced. But it is not in the least Christian.

Here, in *Antigone,* one by one the victims of the tragedy go into the dark. It is all over for Antigone, and Creon can now continue to wait for his own death. "Only the guards are left and none of this matters to them." They go on playing cards. It is very noble to stand by your commitments, to honor your word and so on—and to do so gives a certain dignity to life. Certainly Creon's life is one without dignity or worth. But really is it all justified? A worried administrator going on with the committee work, and a group of soldiers at the death place, dicing or playing cards. *Finis.*

It is not a question of darkness over the land for three hours. The darkness is permanent. No veil is rent, and our only consolation must be that Antigone has done what Antigone desired to do, and that it was nobly desired.

For this purpose the play is perfectly constructed, the characters clear as marble, the contained, cold language flawlessly attuned to the mood. It is courageous and serious and strong; and utterly without joy.

Pause for a moment to think of what Eugene O'Neill would have made of it and you will see the debt owed to the French theatre in purifying the dramatic style when dealing with the high serious moments of human life.[7] The agility of apprehension, the proliferating invention, the

[7] *Three Plays* by O'Neill were published by Vintage Books, 1960.

superb showmanship of O'Neill cannot disguise the fact that he has no philosophy of suffering; neither Christian, classical, nor humanist. He is obsessively drawn to write about suffering, but he writes from no assured center in himself. So when he too takes a classical theme and tries to write an *Oresteia* in terms of a New England household, he produces *Mourning Becomes Electra,* whose style is inflated and unreal. The inflation and unreality result from a dodging of the relation between suffering and faith. In *Lazarus Laughed,* he tries to make a statement about death that would, if accepted, eviscerate the whole dignity of man, and reduce all heroism to a mockery, for the Deity as shown us (by Lazarus at the point of death) is no more than a terrible practical joker—and the laughter of Lazarus neither a lyrical gaiety, nor the abandonment of joy, but a convulsion, a rictus, of horror. The relationship of artistic form to faith or conviction is not a new subject in literary criticism; to read Camus' *Les Justes* and Whiting's *Marching Song,* reinforced by a thimbleful of O'Neill, brings out forcefully what our problem is in this particular case.

O'Neill, uncertain and passionate, bumbles about in a void, his heroes and heroines sleeping with and slaying each other in a fine nonsensical frenzy; and he puts forth a monstrous brood of demon-ridden subhuman creatures really bearing no relation to man as he is, or even as he wants to be, only as he fears to be in nightmare or hangover when the *Iceman Cometh* and day is far off. Yet though O'Neill fears the nothingness, he lacks the courage to proclaim it as the French existentialist theatre proclaims it, and so the size necessary to a work of art is never attained.

67

Whiting's is a more tentative talent; faith is not granted him—but he shows more courage and more humility than O'Neill, and more compassion than Anouilh. Perhaps he died too soon to have mastered the great injunction of Racine, "put nothing upon the stage but what is very necessary." But he had, fundamentally, a Christian approach to the problem of responding to life, of accepting suffering so that new life can grow from the acceptance, and this is evident even in his macabre play *The Devils*.

There is a passage in Jean Louis Barrault's *Reflections on the Theatre* [8] which throws light on what Anouilh has succeeded in doing, on what Camus failed to do, and on what Whiting was trying to do. Barrault is talking about the "shaking up" of a classical theme by a modern playwright and stresses the point that this "shaking up" of a classic demands the power to impose a new pattern on the broken pieces after the jolt has occurred. This can only be done by someone who is in direct touch with the center from which the original classic was created, someone who can restore concentratedness to the theme. O'Neill never found a center at all, and Whiting was still unsure of his center. So one is forced to admit that the Frenchman is the most accomplished dramatist of the three and the one in whom tone, form, character, and language all cohere. Nevertheless, for our study, Whiting with his deeper understanding of the nature of hope and of the response of faith, and with his deeper concern for affirming life, remains of the three the most important writer.

[8] English Translation (London: Barriet Rockliff, 1951.)

In the search for integrity through commitment, apart from differences in the treatment of suffering, there is another difference to be recognized: that between the Christian and the classical concepts of honor.

Shakespeare, in numberless lines, shows that he equates honor with integrity, with being what you are. It is the quality that makes you *you*. "Who steals my purse steals trash, but he that filches from me my good name . . ." The theft deprives you of your status as a man. This theft, or degradation, the heroic man is bound to resist or revenge. The demand at the lowest involves an eye for an eye. At its highest it demands that man be his own conqueror—and failures in self-conquest, equally with all forced submission to others, are derogatory to honor, and unendurable to the truly heroic mind.

In the French classical tragedy, added to this concept of honor there is the further and corollary concept of *la gloire* —the legitimate acclamation which a man may enjoy (and again must safeguard) for the heroic acts he has performed. To dishonor yourself is to fall below your own picture of yourself, your own imaged reputation. In classical tragedy, whether Greek or French, both honor and glory are necessary ingredients in the make-up of the good and great man.

Now what meaning is the Christian to attach to the concept of honor and the pursuit of glory?

Paul gives as Christ's distinctive characteristic that he emptied himself of "glory" and made himself of "no reputation." We see here a fundamental difference between classic and Christian. The Christian glory, the Christian honor is found in union with God, and in any characteristic of man's which bears witness to the nature of God. And what happens to the man, or what the world thinks of the man, or what the man thinks of himself is of no significance at all. Christ did not make himself of evil reputation. He made himself of no reputation. It simply wasn't worth attending to.

In the plays considered above, Antigone is strictly classical. She has elected to act as herself. So has the hero of *Les Justes*. Antigone "finds quarrel in a straw," and the play is ennobled by her fortitude in meeting her doom.

Whiting's hero, Forster, is more subtly delineated. Originally his honor drew all its sustenance from the legitimate acclamation of his men for the heroic *acts* he performed. But in the moment of truth when "like a lover" he drew the child's head down on his shoulder and shot it, something other than the classical ideal broke into his terms of reference—he knew himself other than the sum of his acts. He ceased to be heroic and became human. He recognized his kinship with the weakest human being "dirty, brave, fearful—and alive." And Whiting shows us what Dido Morgen recognizes—that there is now no point in Forster's remaining here. He has done what the skull in the bronze helmet didn't succeed in doing—he has broken out, not out of the trappings of war, but out of the defenses of the hero. He is now open to the future. Brief though that future is, we see the change in him. "You must feel guilty," Bruno says, and Rupert answers, fearlessly, in complete resignation to absolute loss of reputation: "I do."

4
HERE WE ARE

Some Plays About Communication

The negative necessity "to say no, and die" will of course not satisfy man. We are here, and the vast majority of us, even those committed to the doctrine of the absurd, wish to stay here for the period of our natural lives. Our own survival is one of the foci of an anxiety. We wish to lighten, if we can, the darkness that surrounds us. And for this purpose we talk—incessantly it sometimes seems—about our "predicament." If man is not solely the sum of his acts nor the image he has created of himself, what is he and how does he establish the fact that he is? The "predicament" is a constant, but the mode of our communication on the subject is a variable.

Shakespeare, of course, was concerned with this question; man, "the quintessence of dust," was his perpetual study. Yet the drama of his day was geared to doing rather than to being, and he had to throw in a good measure of violent doing to balance the speculative passages in his plays. In the last ten years a great change has taken place in this respect. Only recently, in the plays of Beckett, Ionescu, Genet, Pinter, do we find an audience invited to attend (without beauty of rhetoric, beauty of decor, or aesthetic seductions of any kind) a naked inquiry into the being of man. And one of the factors dividing the theatregoing world into those whose attention is held and those who are

71

bored by these playwrights, is an interest or disinterest in the study of what man is.

John's Gospel tells us that, if we believe in Christ, we are sons of God, here to do what is pleasing to the Father, and that if we please him we shall not notice death. "Heirs, through hope, of everlasting life," says Paul. Now listen to Jean, out of John Osborne's play *The Entertainer*:

> Here we are, we're alone in the Universe, there's no God, it just seems that it all began by something as simple as sunlight striking a piece of rock. And here we are. We've only got ourselves. Somehow, we've just got to make a go of it.

When we read a speech like Jean's we have to agree that the language of John or Paul is without meaning to the midtwentieth century. Even for those who have been brought up on it, it has a surface-meaning rather than a depth-meaning. As communication with those to whom the Christian wishes to speak, it is almost useless. Professor Ronald Gregor Smith writes:

> The struggle is round man himself, and an understanding of what he is. What we are concerned with, therefore, is the search for a new anthropology, a view of man, which will pay proper respect both to the insights of the Renaissance about man and the insights of Christianity about God in relation to man . . . "The knight of faith," as Kierkegaard called him in a beautiful image, can no longer come prancing into the tournament in the panoply of absolute assurance. Absolute solicitude, yes; and absolute resignation. For he comes not from another world but in the new hope and

strength which he is given in this world because of what has been done in and for this world. Like his master, he is the servant, so far as he may be, of men. . . . Everything that man undertakes he does in virtue of the things and people coming towards him from outside himself. He did not make them, he did not think of them, he did not ask for them: they are there, in their own right of existence. Man is made by his free acceptance, in unlimited openness, of what comes to him out of the surrounding darkness.[1]

Antigone and *Marching Song* are two plays that attempt to show us what happens when a man or woman gives in to expedient solutions and acts contrary to a known good; and then what happens when, reaching the limit either of collaboration with evil, or of complacence in the face of self-knowledge, the hero or heroine stands firm.

Anouilh in *Antigone* showed us the heroine standing in the "panoply of absolute assurance," but Whiting's hero, Rupert Forster, and the girl Dido are (in Gregor Smith's words) "made by the free acceptance in unlimited openness of what comes to (them) out of the surrounding darkness." By this free acceptance they release in others a life that can flow once again towards the future.

These two plays are both concerned with the fate of characters who at least aspired to heroic action; and both were involved in destinies larger than their own. The plays immediately to be considered set the problem of "Who am I, Who are you?" in more purely personal, more individualistic terms, dealing with ordinary people in ordinary situations.

[1] *The New Man,* (London: SCM Press, 1956), pp. 59-60.

In his preface to *A View from the Bridge* [2] Arthur Miller contrasts the American social play with the Greek. He asserts that the basic difference between present-day American drama and the Greeks is that for most modern plays the single theme is *frustration*. The individual, once conscious of his identity, is doomed to frustration. The tragic victory is always denied the playwright, Miller believes, because no play can project with any conviction what the society of his time has failed to prove.

Miller continues: "In Greece, the tragic victory lay in demonstrating that whatever the doom of the protagonists, the *polis* had discovered some aspect of Universal Law which also was the right way to live together." After a side glance at Russia, Miller states that each great war in history has turned men further from preoccupation with man, and drawn men further back from the contemplation of universal law, successively into family, home, private life, and eventually into preoccupation with sexuality. (Even if it is a statement of less universal application than he would wish us to believe, Miller's thesis is certainly well exemplified in Edward Albee's play *Who's Afraid of Virginia Woolf?*) We have now, Miller maintains, no character who can stand, in the drama, as the tragic *Questioner*. Our common sense reduces those who do question to the status of misfit, of complainer. Our social aim, our "happiness," is to stay out of trouble. And our deep moral uneasiness, our sense of being only tenuously joined to the others is caused, Miller believes, because a person only has value as he fits into the pattern of *efficiency*.

[2] (New York: The Viking Press, 1962.)

Miller continues: "What we must now know and act upon is that the acceptance of such a sealed fate is to be *resisted*. The Greeks were all in the same boat—their *polis*. We, now, must (like Greek drama, then) ask the largest questions. Where are we going now that we are all together, all in the same boat?"

Out of this preface of Miller's arise several queries. Is the intellectual's present enthusiasm for drama due at all to the decay of satisfying religious ritual? Is Miller right in thinking our society disregards human dignity more than other ages have disregarded it? What about the Helots? What about the galleys? What about Bedlam? And *are* we, in fact, all together in the same boat? Miller is, after all, a playwright, not a sociologist. What does his *play* show us?

A View from the Bridge has, as chorus, a lawyer, one Alfieri, who tells us he came from Sicily originally; a man who has left a country where the original Greek idea of law as beneficent had become debased, in order to come to "a civilized country" (close by Brooklyn Bridge) where another kind of debasement is practiced, the debasement of the half-committed. "Here," says Alfieri, "here we settle for half, and I like it better." And with skillful irony Miller proceeds to show us the passion of Eddie Carbone, the Italo-American, who would not settle for half.

After Eddie's death in a fight, Alfieri speaks the Epilogue thus:

Most of the time we settle for half and I like it better. But the Truth is holy, and even as I know how wrong he was, and his death useless, I tremble, for I confess that something perversely pure calls to me from his memory—not purely good, but himself purely, for he allowed himself to be wholly known and for that I think I will love him more than all my sensible cheats. And yet it is better for settle for half, it must be. And so I mourn him, I admit it, with a certain—alarm.

"With a certain alarm." Yes, indeed. For Eddie surely is man in a void. And if this is a true picture of the plight of the rebel against organization man, there is indeed cause for alarm.

Miller does not show here, and possibly does not in any of his plays, that there is a third alternative. Man may be totally conformed to this world; or he may offer himself, a despairing and death-seeking rebel against "settling for half," or he may take another attitude.

But before attempting to speak of the third alternative, let us see what other playwrights show us about what Miller calls "the fracturing of man's need for union with his society," and the question of establishing a man's own identity, his integrity, so that this image of himself, his identity, is not totally destroyed. We have seen this struggle to preserve identity as treated by a Frenchman, an Englishman, an American. Let us now look at an Australian play, Ray Lawler's *Summer of the Seventeenth Doll*.[3]

Here are two sugarcane cutters, Barney and Roo, and two women. For seventeen summers, at the end of the sugar harvest, the men have come south to a house where their two women live all the year round. The play begins at the point where the game is over. The four men and women know in their hearts that age has caught up with them.

[3] © 1957 by Ray Lawler. Reprinted by permission of Random House, Inc., New York, New York.

They have lived on the purely sensual plane all these years. Hard, monotonous, exhausting physical toil in the fields most of the year for the men; boring, confined, low-status city work for the women, relieved only by a booze-sodden, sex-ridden, animal "lay-off." They finish as they began, animals, dumb in the face of frustration, hardly able to communicate anything of their unhappiness, even to each other.

Roo, whose physical strength has proved inadequate to the labors of the sugar market and who sees himself ousted by a younger man as leader of the cutters' gang, offers Olive marriage and says he will settle down in the city, but Olive violently refuses him. She is another who, in spite of her silly behavior in this, the only important relationship of her whole tiring restricted life, will not settle for half. And when Roo says "This is the dust we're in and we're gonna walk through it like everyone else for the rest of our lives," Olive rejects this travesty of their former glory. Survival is not enough.

A case can be made out for Tennessee Williams in *Cat on a Hot Tin Roof* [4] (as in other plays) that he is a writer concerned to discover what, if anything, there is in man beyond mere sexuality. *Cat*, particularly, presents an inquiry into what the effect upon a family is, of the practice of lying—from whatever motive. Each of them— Brick, Big Daddy, Big Momma, Maggie the Cat, and the visiting relations—builds a wall of lies that, while meant to defend the timid personality from the rapacious and destructive comments of the rest of the family, achieves in the

[4] (New York: New Directions, 1955.)

end only the isolation of each individual within a repellent outer crust, a crust which inhibits any possibility of true human relationship and is the very opposite of Dido Morgen's openness to the future. It is partly because Williams' heroine, Maggie, for all her defects of character, sees that for her to have a child will do far more than ensure the inheritance for Brick and herself, that this play of Williams' has a quality of hopefulness lacking in most of his work. There is at least a willingness to admit the future. For Williams, too, survival is not enough. There must be communication and there must be mutual recognition of identity.

The conjoint problem of identity and communication underlies many of the plays of Eugene Ionescu, who does not rely only on language for the delivery of his message, but makes things speak for him. Nothing is said about the supernatural; everything that happens is "real," yet all is imbued with an interior reality. Ionescu holds that people talk to exist; silence frightens them. And for him language is an escape from reality. The end of the play *The Chairs*,[5] after the old couple have committed suicide, is a stage covered by a jungle of thirty-five chairs, and "the message," which has at last been delivered, has no human hearers.

In *Amédée,* the fact that the love of the married couple had died is symbolized by the presence in their apartment of a corpse which grows and grows. In *The Lesson,* the new victim is coming up the stairs as the latest corpse is carried out. In *The Bald Prima Donna,* the inane conversation is just beginning all over again when the curtain falls. In *Rhinoceros* the human beings begin one after the

[5] (Evergreen ed. New York: Grove Press, 1958.)

78

other to turn into rhinoceroses. Beastly, but Ionescu certainly communicates. An interview in *Encore* quotes him, as saying that "as he is not alone in the world, and as each of us is, deep down, everyone else, one man's dreams, longing, anxieties and obsessions do not belong to him alone. They are part of an ancestral heritage. . . . "It is this," he says, "that constitutes our profound one-ness and our universal language." He does not say, but it is a legitimate corollary, that if we are one with each other in this purely mechanistic mode, we have written *finis* to all moral judgment of man by man and indeed to all ethical awareness. Ionescu does not imagine for a moment that he can save humanity but he is intensely aware of our solitariness, and his concern is to drive us deeper down than the surface ripples on which most of our sailing is done. In the deep is unity.

John Osborne's two first plays captured the public attention, but it is equally significant that he has so far failed to fulfill his promise. In *Look Back in Anger* [6] Alison and Jimmy Porter, and Jimmy's friend Cliff, are penned up together in their attic. Jimmy Porter is, granted, intolerable. But he lives. "Let's pretend we're human beings, let's pretend we're alive," he says. What he has against his wife Alison is that she has always taken life at secondhand. At the moment the play starts Alison knows she is pregnant. But she fears to tell Jimmy. And Jimmy in ignorance says, as he bullies her: "If only she would become human," and

---

[6] (Great Meadows, N. J.: S. G. Phillips, Inc. [1957].) For the background, see J. R. Taylor, *Anger and After: A Guide to the New British Theatre*, now in Penguin Books.

then thinking of what *could* bring her to face life directly, adds: "If she could have a baby and it would die." "Perversely pure," in Miller's words, he *desires* Alison's salvation.

Jimmy wants maturity for himself and for her, but he does not know how or where to start looking for it. Finally, when they are reunited, he takes Alison in his arms and they finish, as Alison feared they would, "rather mad, slightly satanic, very timid little animals, all love and no brains." They are back where they started. But they are now together. Something has been achieved.

At the point where Alison leaves Jimmy, her friend Helena arrives, and in spite of the fact that to do so goes all against her traditional Anglican upbringing, Helena readily lives in sin with Jimmy until she gets tired of it. While her physical passion for Jimmy lasts, no principles deter her. And indeed she learns *something* from her experience. But she represents, as Alison in her way at first represents, a desire to keep herself unspotted from the world, which, in Osborne's view, is the sin of sins, because it is the self-preserving instinct, the negation of human participation in life's wholeness. Helena withdraws from the situation because in it she can't be happy. They all want to escape from the pain of being alive; this is Osborne's complaint against us.

The theme is the same in *The Entertainer*.[7] A weak despair predominates over a strong desire for approval and success, both to be gained without the pain of being alive. Osborne, like Miller, like Lawler, like Williams, like Ionescu, shows us his "little animals" with considerable

[7] (Great Meadows, N. J.: S. G. Phillips, Inc., 1958.)

wit, and so they make good entertainment. But underlying all this, and discounting the obvious bid for the audience's pity, what *is* the anger of Osborne?

The anxiety about identity is certainly not very new, nor the sense of isolation. As Osborne's own play about him proclaimed, these are both parts of Luther. Both experiences preoccupied the minds of Keats and Coleridge; and since poets have always been concerned with problems of being, as opposed to problems of doing, it may be profitable to consider briefly Keats's pursuit of what he calls the "Shape of Beauty."

It is legitimate to equate this Shape of Beauty with what a writer today would probably term "ultimate reality." To Keats the Shape of Beauty is what "moves away the pall/ From our dull spirits." In tracing Keats's investigation into the nature of this movement one finds that he begins with the beauties of the tangible visible world when he stands "tiptoe upon a little hill;" then he comes to regard these natural beauties as an expression of something other. He describes them as "Huge cloudy symbols of a high Romance," as symbolic, we now would say, of an encounter; he passes to acceptance of the need to be "in thrall" to beauty herself, to *La belle dame sans merci,* the reality behind the natural appearances; and finally he comes face to face with the demand which the search for this reality makes upon a man, the demand for surrender, for loss even of identity, even for the abandonment of the *real self*. It is arguable that Keats's progress was really progress along the path of the religious contemplative, a path which begins with self-regard, moves thence to apprehend the reality informing the material world (ourselves included therein), thence to the need to be in thrall to that informing reality and finally to the Pauline condition of total surrender of identity—"I live, yet not I . . ." Absurd? Yes, certainly absurd: and of this more later.

No one would suggest that Keats attained the last stages —poets generally have the wit to stop well short of sanctity. But the comparison breeds hope, for reasons which will shortly emerge.

Those who have been brought up in a Puritan tradition can easily get put off, in the study of the contemporary drama, by the violence and brutality of the stories, by the emphasis upon raw sex (homo- or hetero-), by the generally sordid and unedifying lives of the characters portrayed. We must look deeper to find what the dramatists are really prophesying about. Continuing to use Keats as mentor, consider what he wrote when faced with a vocation too difficult for him:

> My spirit is too weak. Mortality
> Weighs heavily on me, like unwilling sleep.
> And each imagined pinnacle and steep
> Of Godlike hardship tells me I must die
> Like a sick eagle, looking at the sky.

And how do the men and women in Ray Lawler's *Summer of the Seventeenth Doll* describe their plight?

Pearl: Who wants to knit a sweater for an eagle?
Olive: I don't remember calling Roo an eagle.
Pearl: You did, you turned to me and said: "O yes, that's what they remind me of, two eagles, flying down out of the sun and coming south every year for the mating season."

And when the party is finally over, Roo says:

> No more flyin' down outa the sun. No more eagles. This is
> the dust we're in, and we're gonna walk through it like every-
> one else, for the rest of our lives.

"Like a sick eagle looking at the sky." More than a
hundred years ago, poor, silly, suffering Jimmy Porter
speaks in his forerunner John Keats, when Keats struggles
to express something for which there really aren't words,
only *attitudes*. The struggle is to accept "glory." You can't
do much about glory—it dazzles you—that's all.

Keats in writing about his first view of the Elgin marbles
says:

> Such dim-conceivéd glories of the brain
> Bring round the heart an indescribable feud;
> So do these wonders a most dizzy pain
> That mingles Grecian grandeur with the rude
> Wasting of old time—with a billowy main,
> A sun, a shadow of a magnitude.

Jimmy Porter is trying to shoulder the same burden when
he says:

> Was I wrong to believe that there's a—kind of—burning
> virility of mind and spirit that looks for something as power-
> ful as itself? I want a warm, thrilling voice to cry out
> "Alleluia! I'm alive!"

Forgetting for the moment the resurrection language
Jimmy uses, ask yourself whether these two young men
are speaking of anything else but the pain every poet, every

artist, every religious spirit feels when he first must come into the presence of that "shadow of a magnitude" and consequently first recognizes his own identity, knows himself to be

> I, a stranger and afraid
> In a world I never made.

It is not new; though in our age it is perhaps more difficult because of the "fracturing" process which has destroyed the established social framework on which the ordinary man has for long been supported. The nostalgia for the established social structure is often present in today's plays. But a dramatist is not an ordinary man. He needs a different kind of support.

The young artist facing the pain of being alive needs assurance that the shadow is indeed the shadow of a magnitude—not just a gross darkness. Part of our anxiety is that we have lost any confidence in what casts the shadow. Where is the church of Christ in this situation? Surely if anywhere it is in Christ and in his saints that a young man should be able to recognize the burning virility of mind and spirit answering to his own search?

Is Osborne's furious antagonism to the church due to the fact that he knows it ought to have answers for him and, as far as he can see, it offers stones for bread and *cliché* for prophecy? The truly beautiful character of Cliff (whose companionship and whose willingness to "be with" Alison and Jimmy in their self-imposed suffering is one of the permanently memorable achievements of its decade) is contrasted with Helena, the church girl, whose principles stand up to no temptation and whose self-preserving instinct is the dominant factor in her character.

Keats cannot help us here to find out what might offer a solution, for Keats died too young. He was feeling towards an answer in the poem *Hyperion,* but he never completed it. We shall have to look for help to an older man. And Coleridge is the poet who has gone into this, right to the bottom.

In *The Ancient Mariner* the Mariner shoots the albatross, the crew's bird of love. He does this out of ignorance. So here is a man faced with an intolerable situation, isolated from his fellows. For this, if he is responsible, he is responsible through ignorance not through deliberate intent. How does he escape from his predicament? He is led (through the compassion of the Queen of Heaven) to a new vision of life by the experience of joy at the beauty of the water snakes. No doubt the Freudians can explain this in terms of a sublimated sexuality. All the Mariner knows is that simply by a movement of joyful thankfulness towards his fellow creatures, the water snakes, he is released from his ghastly burden.

> The self-same moment I could pray;
>   And from my neck so free
> The Albatross fell off, and sank
>   Like lead into the sea.

The four verses that follow contain the most precise, almost clinical, description of the effects of absolution that anyone is likely to write—dew, sleep, rain, lightness. The becalm'dness was broken. The Mariner was "whole, human, alive—and alone." Does it remind you of Rupert Forster's description in *Marching Song* of his own "becoming human"? He had to wait after that experience—as Paul had to wait after the Damascus road. But though the Mariner is restored to himself, he still cannot reestablish contact with his fellows,

> The many men, so beautiful,
> And they all dead did lie.

They are still dead and he still cannot communicate with them.

> The body of my brother's son
> Stood by me, knee to knee.
> The body and I pulled at the rope
> But he spoke no word to me.

Survival is not enough. There must be communication. So what does he do? He takes the conventional path as soon as he can. He seeks out someone equipped to perform the recognized rite for restoring an outcast into the community again.

Coleridge's lyrical sureness of touch is our guide here— the declension from the tremendous or delicate rhythms of the poem hitherto is cruelly abrupt. Fine cadences do not issue from satirical indignation. We rattle into the description of the "hermit good" who "lives in the wood"— i.e., cut off from normal human intercourse in the busy world:

> He singeth loud his goodly hymns
> That he makes in the wood—
> He'll shrive my soul, he'll wash away

The Albatross's blood—
He kneels at morn and noon and eve,
He hath a cushion plump.
It is the moss that wholly hides
The rotted old oak stump.

A fair description of the church of Christ? Hardly; but Coleridge, like Osborne's Jimmy Porter, like Miller's Eddie Carbone, was in pain and darkness. The Mariner seeks to be so shriven that he can once more be as other men. He seeks absolution and penance. It is something he must have, and something he is confident the hermit has to give. And the "hermit good" has not the remotest idea what the Mariner is talking about, nor where he has been, nor what he needs! Crossing his own brow for safety, the "hermit good" flees out of the story, the Mariner is left alone, and, in Coleridge's note, "The Penance of Life falls on him."

In *The Entertainer* Osborne too has a point to make. He tries to make it in Act I when Archie Rice comes home a bit drunk and agonizedly anxious about his boy Mick, prisoner in enemy hands. Rice starts to tell his daughter Jean a story about two nuns he met on the seafront years ago, a story he says which was "the biggest compliment" he was ever paid. He cannot, in the end, manage to complete the story —but later, when Archie is again drunk, and nearer to his last degradation, and perhaps therefore less sensitive (or perhaps therefore more desperate for understanding?), he tells the story.

Did I ever tell you my Nun's Story? They just took one look at me—and together, at the same time, quite, quite spontaneously, they crossed themselves. They crossed themselves!

87

When before them stands a human soul in mortal sin, and in mortal, desperate need, the Christians cross *themselves* for safety. Osborne tells us the way it might be in Archie's final story of the saint in heaven. He describes there a way of acceptance of each other: a wholly new kind of "togetherness."

This study has led us to review the share which Christians have in the darkness over much of the theatre and over much of the world today. There has been too much behavior like that of Helena in *Look Back in Anger* and the nuns in *The Entertainer*; not enough like the saint in Archie Rice's story. We ought to be grateful to the playwrights who make an amusing evening's entertainment for us out of a conducted tour of their private hells. Miller describes the church in *A View from the Bridge*. In his deep anxiety about Eddie, the lawyer, Alfieri, even went to consult an old lady, a "very wise old woman." All she could do was nod her head and say: "Pray for him." The church of Christ seen from Brooklyn Bridge is an old lady, nodding her head, and with no "practical" solutions to problems of life and death; for one of our failures is a failure to demonstrate the practicalness of prayer—or to demonstrate it all wrong. Hear Jimmy Porter, speaking to Cliff:

> I suppose you're going over to that side as well. Well, why don't you? Helena will help to make it pay off for you. She's an expert in the New Economics—the Economics of the Supernatural. It's all a simple matter of payments and penalties. She's one of those apocalyptic share pushers who are spreading all those rumours about a transfer of power.

That is how we look from outside—still concerned with the transfer of power—still dodging the pain of love.

Reading the gospels as Christians, we put ourselves on the side of the Christ. But if you think of us as the religious people, the conformists, what do you see? A sizeable mob, fellow-traveling like fun, so long as the central Figure keeps on with the loaves and the fishes and the healing miracles. We want to follow, of course. It is inspiring to follow Mr. Eliot into the historic cathedral, with those beautiful words to reassure one. It is still fairly fashionable to stay, with Mr. Eliot again, near the cocktail bar, wincing sensitively at the story of the Crucifixion, retold just horrifically enough, but not in any way that would make one have to leave one's theatre seat. But remember it was a younger Eliot who also wrote:

After such knowledge, what forgiveness?

Stay back, in imagination, a moment longer in Jerusalem with a wretched tiny group of frightened Jews, in Osborne's words "rather mad, slightly Satanic, very timid little animals." Perhaps few Christians of today would have been witnesses of Good Friday; we should have been up at the Temple doing the right thing. Yet the group on Calvary were aware of something which we have overlooked. For no reason now but loyalty (for it was now evident there was nothing in the Kingdom story), they were prepared at least to try to endure the pain of loving; and they were going to fail. And the protagonist? the hero? the man who had willed to become fully human? He was going uphill, with a burden on his back, his face still set like a flint, to die "in absolute solicitude and absolute resignation," in complete openness to whatever was coming to him out of the surrounding darkness, with an unanswered question on his lips.

Peter found it all but impossible to believe there could be any forgiveness, any reinstatement. This is where some of our playwrights are. They are playing for tremendous stakes. They are prepared to be wholly known—at whatever cost. But when they fail, as humanly they will fail, the church as it now stands has no word of absolution which they can understand or accept. We may know, but we do not succeed in communicating what we know. If we could find this key to the word of absolution for our age, the word that strengthens for the penance of life, we would indeed have something to offer the Great Theatre of the World.

In Auerbach's *Mimesis* there is a translation of a letter sent by Francis of Assisi to one of his brethren who was having a rough time. Francis writes: "Love those who obstruct your path, love them for this and do not desire that they be better Christians." It is an exhortation not to leave the world behind but to mingle with its torment and to endure evil with passionate devotion. Someone has got to take on this truly Franciscan vocation, someone who has spent a long while thinking about what it takes to be a prophet. No one has been able to tell these playwrights that all a prophet can hope to hear are the words: "Son of man, stand upon your feet." The grief is that there exists the whole glorious company of the prophets standing around them, and not one of us is properly equipped to effect an introduction.

Yet, if we study contemporary plays with an open Testament—Old or New—alongside the text, and cultivate a kind of childish attentiveness, we may become a little more understanding of what we have to learn from the playwrights and what we very possibly have to offer them for their strengthening. We may learn how to convince them and their audiences that Resurrection is a word which has meaning; that for them the choice is not simply either to give in and conform, or to rebel and despair. The third alternative is to become one with other people, as concerned, as committed, as they are, as naked to criticism, as sensitive to contempt and to failure, as much in the dark, as open to the future; exactly as they are except for one fact —the certainty that the voice they long to hear has been, and can be, heard, the voice of Someone who did not ever "settle for half," but whose definitive utterance might for our day be translated into Osborne's words: "Alleluia! I'm alive!"

5

END GAME

*Some Plays about the Possibility
of Resurrection*

Can the contemporary theatre echo with any sound re-
motely like an Easter *Alleluia?* Greek drama began in the
rite of renewal, the spring festival. The Christian drama
of the Middle Ages was born as the women's coming to the
empty tomb was reenacted in the churches. But with the
emphasis so rightly falling on the integrity of a modern
person, can the serious playwright of today concern himself
in any way with the Christian doctrines of atonement, redemption, and resurrection? In this last chapter we shall
briefly examine two plays which seem consonant with an
orthodox Christian view of man—Christopher Fry's *The
Dark Is Light Enough* and Henri Bernanos' *The Carmelites*
—before looking at two other plays by Samuel Beckett,
plays which are more typical of the "new" theatre, and
which will lead us to an uncertain conclusion.

The heroine of *The Dark Is Light Enough,*[1] Countess
Rosemarin Ostenburg, is, like Catherine de Troyes in
Whiting's *Marching Song,* shut up in her wintry "castle,"
somewhere in Austria with a group of hangers-on; but
Fry's play reaches out beyond the enclosing walls more
than Whiting's does. The countess is free to act, even if
she acts eccentrically. And she has to be matched against

[1] (New York: Oxford University Press, 1954.)

Whiting's Dido Morgen, not against Catherine de Troyes, for Rosemarin, like Dido, is the character who causes change in other lives.

The play opens with two of the hangers-on discussing Rosemarin's latest eccentricity. She has driven off, alone, in her sleigh, early that morning, leaving a note of explanation, which, like most of her explanations, only renders the facts more obscure. Her friends are upset. It is one of her Thursday evenings, and she has not missed a Thursday since—since when?

> *Jakob:* Isn't it true that in more than twenty years
>   She has only once before failed her Thursdays,
>   When her son Stefan was born?
> *Kassel:* Not even once.
>   "Good God," she said, "I think the monkey
>   Means to be born on Thursday evening."
>   But she received us all at seven o'clock,
>   And at nine, when Gyorki was saying, as usual,
>   That there is no clear truth except the present
>   Which alters as we grasp it,
>   She bowed to us in the doorway, and said
>   "We must freely admit the future," and withdrew
>   To give birth to Stefan.

These gossipy men go on building up for us a picture of Rosemarin, which is one of the most delightful of Fry's preparatory scenes. It is evident that Thursdays are for the visitors a kind of religious observance. In spite of winter and war, they are here.

Then they go on to tell us how this great and good lady conscripted her little daughter, then aged seventeen, into a marriage, ten years ago, with a total wastrel of a man,

93

Richard Gettner. Why? At this point the countess returns, her arrival heralded by that of—Richard Gettner! Rosemarin explains that she went out to rescue Richard. All are indignant, the countess gay and unrepentant. From then on the question, which is asked in scenes of mounting intensity, is "What price is the countess prepared to pay for the redemption of Richard Gettner, the lost sheep of the flock?" She offers him one after another of her treasures, her son Stefan now, as she offered her daughter ten years earlier. While yet she does not know whether Richard has only wounded or really killed Stefan, she speaks thus to the sergeant who wants to make Richard "pay":

> Pray for him,
> Not because I love him, but because
> You are the life you pray for. And because
> Richard Gettner is the life you pray for.
> And because there is nothing on the earth
> Which doesn't happen in your own hearts.

Richard Gettner is saved from his enemies, not once but repeatedly, through Rosemarin's intervention. Finally Gettner returns, at great personal risk, to the countess' presence. He has heard she is ill, and he is angry with her for being so. She may think her work is done

> . . . But out here
> The drowning still goes on.

So the final scene is played out between the dying countess, now no more to ascend and descend the great staircase on her heavenly traffic of salvation, and the hunted sinner, who still hopes to possess her in his own right.

Only at the very end, faced with the "absolute No" of
Rosemarin's death, he shows the spark of real devotion
which Rosemarin had willed to persist through all his hate-
ful, hate-filled life. He ceases to run away, and standing,
faces the oncoming enemy.

The Carmelites by Bernanos [2] is a play about fear, but it
is also about honor. In the place of honor and the courage
that supports it, we are shown fear and the grace that over-
comes it.

Two sentences are central to the theme. One is placed on
the flyleaf.

> In one sense, d'you see, Fear really is the daughter of God,
> redeemed on the night of Good Friday. She is present at
> every deathbed, she does intercede for man.

And the other sentence of prime importance is one spoken
early in the play by the old prioress:

> Do not despise yourself. God has taken charge of your hon-
> our. It is safer in his hands than in yours.

Set in France in 1774, the play tells of the persecution
and finally the execution on the guillotine of a small community of Carmelite nuns in Paris. Bernanos explores in
the play the nature of fear and courage as they act and
react upon a close-knit Christian community. The contemporary idea of honor is seen through the eyes of the
worldly ladies of the convent and, opposed to this, the absolute resignation of the fully obedient sister, the absolute
solicitude and responsibility of the Superior of the House.

[2] (London: Wm. Collins Sons & Co., 1961.)

We are shown two prioresses, an old one who dies of illness and her younger successor, who is martyred, and against these conflicting temperaments we see the life and death of Blanche de la Force herself, first as postulant, then as novice.

Blanche has entered the order because she is temperamentally the victim of absolutely insurmountable terror. She is fear personified, and realizes that, coming as she does of noble lineage, she is utterly unfit to comport herself according to the standard of honor her birth demands. In the face of danger, she knows she will always break. Once accepted by Carmel, she learns that even *there* is no refuge for her fearful soul. When her order is threatened by the Revolution, the seniors, Mère Marie and the prioress, debate what is to happen to Blanche. The community takes a vow of martyrdom. What will become of the honor of the community if Blanche fails, as fail she will, to stand up to death on the guillotine? They decide to send her away, and Mère Marie is to go with her. Mère Marie is a fine brave character, worldly in the sense that, to her, honor means what it meant to any man of the period. But her martyrdom is to accept the fact that God has another destiny for her than heroic death. The two nuns, Mère Marie and Blanche, are together when they hear that the sisters are all condemned to die, and now comes the climax of the play, a climax prepared long before—as is the climax in *Marching Song*.

In her early days as a postulant, Blanche was summoned to the bedside of the first prioress of the convent, who was making, religiously speaking, a very bad death. The prioress, a woman of remarkable fortitude, finds herself at the end in a prolonged agony of unrelieved terror. One of the sisters, Constance, says of the prioress' death: "It was as though she was dying someone else's death."

"What do you mean, someone else's death?" asks Blanche, and Constance replies:

> It means that some other, when the hour of death comes, will be astonished at how easily it happens. How—how comfortable she feels in dying. She may even get a little glory out of it. No one dies to himself. We die for each other, perhaps we even die each other's deaths—who knows?

So at the very end when the last Carmelites are making their good deaths, the procession moves slowly up across the square to the guillotine, chanting *Salve Regina,* and *Veni Creator,* and the voices become each moment fewer and fewer, now two and now only one. Suddenly from the far side of the square a new voice is added, clearer, more resolute even than the others, and yet with something child-like in it. And across the square, the crowds parting involuntarily to let her pass, comes Blanche, her face stripped of all trace of fear, and she sings the last stanza of the Carmelite sacrifice:

> *Deo Patri sit gloria*
> *Et Filio qui a mortuis*
> *Surrexit ac Paraclito*
> *In saeculorum saecula.*

She too comes up to the guillotine and her voice, like the voices of all her sisters, is received into the silence.

In these plays the central figures, Gettner and Blanche, are redeemed by the self-offering of others. They bear within them the principle of their own destruction, and have to be transfigured through the sacrificial act of another. The plays, therefore, perfectly conform to Cornford's definition of the ritual comedy, as "at once a sacrifice and a triumph" or feast.[3] In each play we see the sinner—the person who is in danger of missing the mark, if you like that term better—brought out of despair, absolved, loosed from bondage, reinstated.

Blanche de la Force says early in the play: "You can't know your own value unless you have some touchstone to prove it against." The heroism of the sisters of her community gives Blanche this touchstone by which to measure her own ultimate capabilities. She is given also a whole to which her incompleteness can attach itself; the exchange of deaths which the first prioress offers for Blanche's sake, a good example of what Charles Williams calls "co-inherence," enables Blanche to die the courageous death that was really earned, if one may so express it, by the old prioress' life. The reconciliation, the atonement, is vicariously achieved.

Gettner would long since have "ridden into the nightmare," as he says, had not Rosemarin offered for him everything she held most dear; and ultimately, on the earth, her life. Solely by Rosemarin's eccentric way, truth, and life, Gettner, whose heart, brain, and willpower are, he knows, "deserters to the death," is brought to the point where he can stand fast and let in the future. In each case, we witness Easter, which the theologian Rudolf Bultmann well describes as the "rising of faith." "The life of faith," says

[3] Francis M. Cornford, *The Origin of Attic Comedy*.

Bultmann, "is to open ourselves freely to the future. In bringing a man to faith the love of God treats man as other than he is, embraces and sustains him even in his fallen self-assertive state, and so frees him from himself as he is, to be what he was intended to be." This is precisely the service which the women who in these plays are the agents of the love of God perform for Gettner and Blanche de la Force.

In the deepest sense, both *The Dark Is Light Enough* and *The Carmelites* are comedies. Wylie Sypher, in an essay on *Comedy*,[4] refers to the mythological ritual cycle— birth, struggle, death, and resurrection—in connection with the Christian story. Sypher points out that the "narrow arc of tragedy" is limited in its dealings with the theme to the first three moments—birth, struggle, death. Sypher says: "The range of comedy is wider than the tragic range— and perhaps more fearless—and comic action can risk a different sort of purgation and triumph." Is this the reason (he asks) why it is difficult for tragic art to deal with the Christian themes of crucifixion and resurrection? Certainly, religious drama as too often presented is in real danger of developing *rigor mortis* through living always under the shadow of a small but deadly earnestness which dehumanizes both author and audience. This kind of drama springs from the worst kind of didacticism, which stands remote, disapproving, and joyless in the sanctuary, and which preaches instead of participating in the world.

Happiness, for our present purpose, can be considered as the dominant emotion in the musical comedy or fairy tale plot. It consists in conforming to the pattern required

[4] (New York: Doubleday Anchor Books, 1956.)

by one's social group—the plain girl becomes pretty, the poor boy becomes rich, cruel fate becomes kind, and death or disaster never enter the scene at all. Comedy seldom presents happiness untinged by deeper emotion. Probably Wylie Sypher's idea that the comic is able to bear the full weight of human experience ought to be true. It is not quite certain that we can prove it so at the present time. Comedy is certainly more comprehensive than tragedy. The comic artist accepts the improbable as a start—nothing human is foreign to the comic muse. For religious plays we need, however, a vehicle that can reach out beyond what is human at surface level to include what is deepest, most complex and most lofty in human intuition. Comedy here again is a suitable vehicle for the expression of humanity's depths and heights, for comedy is built upon a sacramental view of life, on the ambiguity of all the world of the senses. If we are to have a dramatic medium to express the Christian life of faith, it must be one that admits all the imperfections of the human race and that admits them in order that they may suffer change, as in Ariel's song about the dead king. In this sense of imperfection, together with the longing for completion, lies, in fact, our only hope of a future.

In his book *Answer to Job*,[5] Carl Jung has a definition of "completeness as imperfection, perfection as incomplete," which is very relevant to our subject. Men, Jung says, aim at perfection, women at wholeness or completeness. To wish to be perfect is to deny the whole of the dark side of one's nature, to refuse to recognize the need for grace and redemption. The danger menacing perfectionist man is that

[5] (Meridian Books, New York: World Publishing Company [1954].)

of sterility—perfection once thought to have been achieved, no future, no change, is thinkable. The danger residing in woman's desire for completeness is a lack of selectiveness— everything is as important as everything else. Woman, therefore, while more accessible to sin, is also more open to salvation.

Jung's elucidation of the different attitude of men and women to perfection also throws light upon the question of honor. A man has a static image of himself, his honor, which he regards it as his duty to preserve. The heroic figure preserves this image. The tragic hero falls from it, and this (since tragedy is written exclusively by men) is regarded as a disaster. The hero has incurred dishonor. His perfection has been questioned, denied, demolished. Women, as Jung rightly indicates, have not so much of this perfectionism. They want the whole works: apple, serpent, and all. They know perfection is a lost dream. They know no one will ever be perfect. From aeons of bearing, rearing, and cherishing men, this one thing, inalienably, *they know*. Religiously, this knowledge is of profound importance. For what to T. S. Eliot is "the barely prayable prayer of the One Annunciation," the total "Yes" of Mary to the overshadow- ing of the spirit, is not, to most women, something wholly without precedent. The reader will not misunderstand this. It is not to speak lightly or blasphemously. But the fact is that to make an unconditional assent to the total demand of a new life is the experience of every woman who has will- ingly given birth to a child.

We see in John's Gospel the Mother at the wedding pointing to the Messiah; the much-married woman of Samaria at the well also acknowledging the Messiah; the figure of the adultress used as a reproof of all sinners, bearing her silent testimony to the also silent but blazing power and purity of the Godhead; the sisters Mary and Martha at Bethany, to witness the life-giving power of the Lord at the raising of Lazarus; Mary of Magdala, anointing the Lord against his burial; the wonderful symbol of the Passion, the woman in travail having sorrow, but as soon as she is delivered she knows joy that a man is born into the world—i.e., that the future is admitted; the word from the cross to the Mother and to John that seals the permanent interdependence of the sexes—every woman as much my responsibility as the mother who bore me, every man as much my responsibility as the son I bore; then the preparation for burial of the Lord of Life, performed by the women; finally the Resurrection appearance to Mary of Magdala, hanging around after the sensible men had seen that it was all over. Because of this absurdity in her, to Mary is committed also the first word of reinstatement in the life of grace, the first missionary charge: "Go to my brethren . . ."

If comedy is, as Sypher suggests, the right mode for the dramatic representation of the awe-ful and holy Easter story, why have we so few Resurrection comedies? Do we lack the necessary fearlessness? Do we shun the absurd improbability of life through death? Is our approach too masculine, too perfectionist, too entangled with honor, too proud, to endure, fundamentally, the humiliating idea of vicarious redemption?

At least it is true that, constantly, whatever the plot of a play in this present time, wherever joy appears, it has a redemptive quality, it is associated with a sense of wonder, and it is mediated by a woman. And looking back at the

Gospel of John, one sees that after women have been presented in every relationship to men—mother, wife, harlot, sister, and friend—the role assigned to women by John is that, ultimately, they come together both to close the life in the old dispensation and to open the life of faith to the brethren. They stand as handmaids or mediators of the wonder of the Resurrection. "Go to my brethren . . ."

But it is not easy to go and to tell. Samuel Beckett in his play *Endgame* [6] makes a very important statement about the conditions of resurrection for man today.

In a blank wall are set two tiny windows; against the wall, two dustbins with lids on; a chair like a throne on wheels; a door that leads into a kitchen; another door that leads out; a ladder. The chair is occupied by a being called Hamm, the body covered with a sheet, the face covered with a blood-stained handkerchief. The second human figure, Clov, is occupied in rather aimless activity, looking out of the window or taking the covers off the two dustbins. Hamm, the seated figure, takes the handkerchief from his face, yawns, holds out the handkerchief at arm's length, and one sees that he wears the dark glasses of the blind. One sees also that the handkerchief is an old one, and very interesting, for it is a Veronica handkerchief, reminding us at once of the tradition that when Christ stumbled and fell under the weight of the Cross on the road to Calvary, Veronica, in pity, wiped his face with her kerchief, and the linen ever thereafter bore the miraculous imprint of the features of the Lord.

[6] Written and translated by Samuel Beckett (Evergreen ed. New York: Grove Press, 1958).

This handkerchief is Hamm's. And his first audible words are, in hesitant French, *Peut il y a—y avoir, misère plus haute que la mienne?* "Was ever grief like mine?" He answers himself: "Perhaps long ago—but I mean now?"

The play proceeds. The dustbins hold two remnants of human figures, Nell and Nagg, "cursed progenitors" Hamm calls them. These white ghostly figures of the past are so mutilated that there is no longer any point even in changing the sterile sand in their dustbins.

Hamm and Clov alone remain. In Freudian terms they may indeed be the tyrannous id and the constantly elusive ego, but also and more profoundly they represent the part of man that covets and claims Godhead. This is shown by Hamm in his boastfulness, his desire that at least a toy dog shall exist to adore him, his belief that he provides Clov with a home, and so on. Clov, whose whole function is service, seeks constantly to escape, to "be a beginning," but the light falls only on the blank wall. There is nowhere to go if he goes. Nothing that speaks of the future can enter. Here within walls Clov's seed will not germinate. Outside, there is no female principle, no accepting vessel—only a little boy, and he will either die out there in the zero landscape, or he will enter the walled place and die within it.

At various points in the play Hamm has told a story about a man, the man who comes to the master to ask for work. This story is gradually dropped as the play proceeds, but it is very relevant for it indicates in one more way the central theme of the play—that we are all in this dead end, and that our only hope is in entering more deeply into life, pain, and grief before we seek any personal alleviation.

In the last scene of the play Hamm wants Clov to wrap

him up in the graveclothes again. But Clov refuses—one must not escape from life, however intolerable, into death.

Clov himself tries to make his escape but, in the end, stays. What indeed could he do, alone? Of what use is a Clov, a nail, without Hamm, the hammer? They are parts of a whole. Clov's last speech must be taken together with Hamm's. Clov says, "Sometimes I tell myself, 'Clov, you must manage to suffer better—if you want the punishment to stop.' Sometimes I say, 'Clov, you must *be* there better, if you want to be allowed to depart.'" Here, before Clov falls silent, there is a wonderful interchange of thanksgiving and absolution between Hamm and Clov—a ritual after which there need be no further words between them.

And Hamm (who has earlier told us a story of the man who wanted to be a servant, who has told us that we ought to go out and love each other, "lick each other's wounds"), considers at the last moment what it would mean if "it happened"—if "He" "came down." He questions an absent power. He asks, "Are you prepared for him [the man of the story] to increase while you [O Absent Power] decrease? Yes? Then let us say no more. We are there." What remains? To strip oneself and jettison every last rag of dominance—the whistle, the dog, who is a symbol of man's coveted dominion over the brute creation—till at last nothing is left but the "old rag," the Veronica handkerchief, the sign of human compassion.

Here Beckett has written—far more deeply than Archibald MacLeish in his play *J.B.*—the story of Job's withstanding of God to the last desperate stripping of everything that man normally counts as his life. Relentlessly, the playwright deprives his hammer-nail couple, his two

natures of man, of all their human attributes except *bare life*
and their mutual compassion. He leaves them with nothing
but their compassion for each other. In *Act Without
Words*,[7] Beckett's next play, even that is removed, and man
is shown as enduring, without response, the remorseless
persecution and tormenting of an unseen silent power.
What Beckett is saying to us, with ever increasing intensity,
is the same "lesson" which Camus drove home; namely,
that the courage required of us is the courage to go right
down into despair, not even asking if there is an exit. In
Camus' words the courage required is to examine whether
we can "live with what we *know,* and only with that. . . ."

We are wrong if we regard this attitude as unchristian,
for in the story of Calvary we are shown precisely this stripping, precisely this dereliction, precisely this unshakeable
compassion, precisely this limitation to what can be known.

The only way to change the story, says Hamm, would be
to introduce some new characters. The only way to change
the Christian story, said some disciples, would be to introduce a legion or two of angels. But this is not the way into
resurrection.

Will there be a resurrection for this age of waiting? Will
the theatre itself be renewed in an Easter light? We cannot
say. Anyone who has witnessed *Krapp's Last Tape,*[8]
Beckett's play for one male voice and a tape recorder, may
feel either that the play really represents the end for the
theatre, or that it vindicates Arthur Miller's contention that
the drama has been driven back from considering universal

[7] *Acte sans Paroles* (Paris: Editions de Minuit).
[8] (Evergreen ed. New York: Grove Press, 1960.)

law to concentrating on mere sexuality. There is in Krapp's life nothing which he values except the recollection of sexual intercourse and the transient satisfaction of the banana and the bottle. No human relationship remains; he spits upon his moments of "inspiration." Solipsism has won. There is an unanswered question twice repeated: "Jesus? Jesus? Was he right after all?" Grant-aided middle-brow students attend performances of this play in appreciative silence as Krapp pours forth words of profound despair.

At an experimental theatre in London in the spring of 1964, Artaud's *Theatricalities* were presented, with no words at all. Violence in sound and movement assaults eye and ear. In vast halls all over England the "Liverpool sound" draws the crowds, its beat achieving effortlessly that total involvement of spectator with spectacle so much desired by Max Reinhardt. Around us the decibel level of noise rises month by month: Our eyes are met by action-paintings and assemblages of miscellaneous *objets trouvés*. It is at least questionable whether there is any longer a public for the spoken word except in the seclusion of the home, mediated by the intimate techniques of broadcasting. Titles of plays have achieved a new form. *It's a Mad, Mad, Mad, Mad World; The Milk Train Doesn't Stop Here Any More; A Funny Thing Happened on the Way to the Forum; How to Succeed in Business Without Really Trying; Stop the World, I Want to Get Off*. These are admen's titles, salesmen's drumming. The audience arrives at the theatre already softened up; it is handed a labeled package, with instructions printed outside about the proper reception of the contents, whether or not they are worth consuming. On television, Kennedy's assassination and the subsequent shooting take place before our eyes. The Pope kisses the soil of Gethsemane and we watch the slight trembling of his hands. A moonprobe fails to take its three thousand photographs and we feel rather cheated. With fresh actualities constantly crowding in, the whole Great Theatre of the World sits in a corner of every room; we have only to switch on, in order to see the latest crucifixion, the newest Easter bonnet.

We have reviewed, you might say, a sad twenty years of false starts in the theatre where it touches the area of religion. The revival of poetic drama faded almost before it began. The plays for churches died partly of cold, but ultimately for lack of power or glory. The play of heightened language—Dorothy L. Sayers, T. S. Eliot, Charles Williams—frankly embarrassed the general public, and failed even with the *côterie* in the end, because the naturalistic settings and characterizations were false to the dialogue. At length Beckett's Anglo-Irish split-level consciousness disciplined by French syntax brought the flicker of his double-tongued metaphysical puns to light up for us fresh possibilities of communication, and we hoped to find in his work a language capable of bearing the weight of religious statement in the theatre. The event has shown Beckett without any real religious statement to make.

All this suggests a gloomy prognosis for the theatre where it touches religion. But the "new" theatre has, after all, only just begun. The true line of the theatre is slender perhaps, but the remarkable thing is that today only the best will do for the serious playgoer. There is a public taste which has developed out of all expectation, largely through the experience brought to it by the very mass media that were thought likely to be its destruction. We have made extraordinary strides in critical power. From being a family of Bottom's children, anxious to play everything from Moonshine to Lion, we have become almost overnight a family of Hamlets, prodigal of advice—"Nay, do not saw the air too much with your hand . . . ." This intensely critical spirit is abroad everywhere, expressing itself particularly in satire often brilliantly funny, and demanding extreme virtuosity from its creators.

The same critical spirit permeates the church. Nothing and no one escapes criticism, nor does any one question his own right to an opinion on another's skill, or craft, or character. And the whole trend of our educational system encourages this critical development. In the long run nothing withstands the hail of criticism except sheer vitality, whether physical or spiritual. "I'm alive!" is the statement that claims attention and is the criterion for success.

Two conclusions emerge. One is that in the serious "new" theatre now beginning it is a Christian duty to encourage wherever possible the creative, comedic view, alongside the critical, satirical temper. The play matters more than the critics' analysis. It is the creative Christian life that convinces, in all its generosity, its confusion, its voracity of appetite. This is a moment for the affirmation of images, not for their rejection.

And the second conclusion is this. If affirmation is asked of us, we must affirm valid images and new ones, not merely enshrine the old. We must be ready for our whole known world of symbols to disappear and be replaced. Perhaps, to close this book, one may borrow an image from one of the most powerful plays of the decade—the musical, *West Side Story*. The rival New York gangs are on stage, packed elbow to elbow and knee to knee on the narrow strip of concrete over which their war is being fought. Overhead loom skyscraper tenement flats, their jagged fire escapes crossed by horizontal lines of washing hung up to drip overhead. Noise, heat, exhaustion of nerves: the movements are angular, jerky, subhuman. Suddenly, the two young lovers come together in the crowd. They link little fingers. At the moment of touching, the entire scene is "flown"—the whole sordid menace of buildings disappears and the stage reveals, against a serene horizon, a wide beach, a distant sea, soft evening light. Instantly, the pent-up children spread across the stage, their movements gentle, their faces relaxed, eyes and voices quiet, affectionate. A true human relationship is established, an interchange of love is accomplished—and a world is renewed.

Camus, at the end of *The Rebel*, writes: "Among the ruins, we are all preparing a rebirth, beyond the limits of Nihilism. But few of us know this." Arthur Miller, in his latest play, ends by speaking of the possibility of knowing "and even happily, that we meet unblessed . . . after the Fall" and that "it does seem feasible . . . not to be afraid." [9] The humiliating absurdity of resurrection through death becomes real to us only at the point of despair. In theatre and church renewal will come. But with what body it will come, what word will accompany the moon voyager to the Sea of Tranquility, how many acts we have still to play, in how much time—these questions remain.

[9] Arthur Miller, *After the Fall*, in *Saturday Evening Post*, February 1, 1964.

INDEX

111